W9-BCX-687

DE GAULLE

EUROPEAN PROBLEM STUDIES

Under the editorial direction of
HENRY BERTRAM HILL

DE GAULLE

Anachronism, Realist, or Prophet?

Edited by F. ROY WILLIS

University of California, Davis

HOLT, RINEHART AND WINSTON
New York • Chicago • San Francisco • Toronto • London

Cover illustration: Speech on the Constitution at Place de la République, September 1958. *(Wide World Photos, Inc.—New York)*

Copyright © 1967 by Holt, Rinehart and Winston, Inc.
All Rights Reserved
Library of Congress Catalog Card Number: 67–10598
2560308
Printed in the United States of America

2 3 4 5 6 7 8 9

CONTENTS

CHRONOLOGY

1890   Birth in Lille of Charles-André-Marie-Joseph de Gaulle

1910   Enters French military academy of Saint-Cyr

1913   Joins 33d infantry regiment, commanded by Pétain

1914   Service on Western Front

1916   Captured at Verdun

1919–20   Attached to Weygand mission in Poland; instructor at Polish War School

1921   Marriage to Yvonne Vendroux; professor of history at Saint-Cyr

1922   Advanced training at Senior War School

1924   With army of occupation in Mainz; publishes first book, *La Discorde chez l'ennemi*

1925   Joins Pétain's staff at Superior War Council

1927   With army of occupation in Trier

1929   With general staff of French army, Beirut

1932   Secretary of Superior Council of National Defense; publishes *Le Fil de l'épée*

1934   Publishes *Vers l'armée de métier*

1937   Commands 507th tank regiment at Metz

1938   Publishes *La France et son armée*

1940   May—Commands 4th Armored Division in battles of Moncornet and Laon
       June—Under-Secretary of War in Reynaud cabinet
       June 18—Appeal for continued resistance in London broadcast
       August—Agreement with Churchill on status of Free French

1941   Gaullist forces seize Saint-Pierre—Miquelon

1942   Free French not included in invasion of French North Africa

1943   January—De Gaulle summoned to Casablanca conference
       June—Formation of French Committee of National Liberation (Comité Français de Libération Nationale, CFLN)
       August—Giraud ousted from CFLN

1944   August—Return to Paris
       December—Visit to Moscow

1945   February—Not invited to Yalta conference

1946   Resignation as Premier

1947   Foundation of Rally of the French People (Rassemblement du Peuple Français, RPF)

1953   Disbands the RPF

1954   Publishes first volume of *Mémoires de guerre*

1955   Retires to Colombey-les-deux-Eglises

1958   May—Algerian uprising
       June—Invested as Premier

1959   January—Elected president of the Fifth Republic
       September—Offers Algeria self-determination

1960   Barricades in Algiers

1961   The Generals' revolt in Algiers

1962   March—Evian agreements end Algerian war
       July—Explosion of French atomic bomb

1963   January—Vetoes British entry to Common Market
       Signs Treaty of Cooperation with West Germany

1964   Tours Latin America

1965   July—Orders temporary French boycott of European Communi
       December—Re-elect President

INTRODUCTION

Early in 1965, a prominent French weekly carried on its front page a photograph of a satisfied President Charles de Gaulle surrounded by pictures of Stalin, Roosevelt, and Churchill. The biting caption was: "Alone at last." The Big Three, who had refused to admit de Gaulle to the handling of the world's problems at Teheran and Yalta, were all dead, while de Gaulle, at 74 years of age, was President of a France more prosperous, populated, and powerful than at any time in its history. His world stature was undeniable, his career universally recognized as controversial but of historical significance.

The first four groups of readings in this book cover the main phases of de Gaulle's career: theorist of tank warfare, 1932–1939; head of the Free French and Premier of liberated France, 1940–1946; leader of the unsuccessful Rally of the French People (Rassemblement du Peuple Français, RPF), 1947–1953; and, since 1958, last Premier of the Fourth and first President of the Fifth Republic. The final group of readings asks the question, What kind of man is de Gaulle? The readings have been chosen to illustrate several different approaches to interpretation of de Gaulle's career. There is first the openly adulatory approach of the Gaullist writers, who seek only the favorable interpretation of the General's actions; sometimes this approach comes from genuine hero workship, as is the case with most foreign admirers, but often, in the case of French supporters, as a reinforcement of de Gaulle's political position in France by creation of a Gaullist Legend similar in effect to the Napoleonic Legend that helped bring Louis Napoleon Bonaparte to power in 1848. The second approach is that of the passionately involved critic. French writers of this type are often outraged at de Gaulle's internal policies, while other Europeans are disturbed at the effects of his foreign policy, especially his attitude to European integration. Finally, there are the dispassionate professional observers, such as some French political scientists and journalists, whose judgments exert an important influence on French public opinion, and foreign scholars, often American or British, who provide some of the most valid comment on the contemporary French scene.

The reader will find that the authors of the selections given here are continually asking three basic questions: Is de Gaulle out-of-date, a leader who is attempting to apply the conceptions of an earlier age in the twentieth century? Or is he acutely aware of immediate problems and necessities and bending his attitudes and policies to meet them? Or is he a man with a mission, to prepare his fellow men for a future into which he alone has insight? Is he, in short, an anachronism, a realist, or a prophet?

By most tests, de Gaulle had achieved little of lasting significance before the outbreak of World War II. In 1939 he was only a colonel; he had written a few small books, suggesting in one that a great commander should know the moment when to disobey his superiors and in another proposing that France equip itself with a mobile force of six tank divisions. He had been favorably noticed by some of the leading politicians of the Third Republic, including Léon Blum and Paul Reynaud, and had brought himself into disfavor with several army leaders, particularly Weygand and Pétain. Yet within nine months, he was to denounce the legally invested government of France and win for himself the acclaim of the French people not only as the source of authority but as the savior of their honor. The significance of his early years of apparent failure lay in preparing de Gaulle for this role.

De Gaulle himself claims that his early upbringing was of vital importance in forming his aims and ideals. He was born in the northern industrial town of Lille in French Flanders, on November 22, 1890. While his family, with some justification, traces its ancestors back to lesser aristocrats who fought the English at Agincourt and received a fief from Philip Augustus, his own parents and grandparents were teachers, philosophers, and historians —deeply patriotic, puritanically Catholic, and strongly intellectual. In his childhood, de Gaulle remarks in the most famous paragraph of his memoirs, he thought of France as "the princess in children's stories or the Madonna of the frescoes," and he became convinced "that France would have to go through great trials, that the purpose of life was to render it some major service one day," and that he would have the opportunity to do so. In 1909 he was accepted as a candidate for the officers' training academy of Saint-Cyr; he spent one year in the ranks as required by law and then two years at the academy, from which he graduated in the top ten. In 1913 he chose to join the 33d infantry regiment from Lille, whose colonel was Philippe Pétain.

The opening of the World War I impressed de Gaulle deeply by healing France's internal divisions. "It is only necessary for France to draw its sword," he wrote later, "for all passions to be aligned." During the first two years of the war he distinguished himself for bravery, was wounded three times, promoted to captain, and on March 2, 1916, captured in the defense of Verdun. Two years of inactivity in German prison camps, from which he tried five times to escape, delayed his advancement in the army; and on his release after Germany's defeat, he sought further action in Poland, serving with General Weygand's mission to the Polish forces in the Russo-Polish fighting of 1919–1920 and taking a direct part in the defense of Warsaw from the Red Army.

De Gaulle then turned to military theory. He taught tactics at the Polish War School and military history at Saint-Cyr, after which he was accepted at the Senior War School for two years of further training in strategy (1922–1924). The fact that he won a mock battle during his training by breaking the rules he was being taught is often cited as the beginning of his struggle with the conservatism of the French general staff and as the reason for his posting outside France with the army of occupation at Mainz. There he revised notes written during his imprisonment on the reasons for Germany's defeat and published them as *Discord among Our Enemies (La Discorde chez l'ennemi)*, his first major literary venture. In 1925 he joined Pétain's staff at the Superior War Council, where he was given the task of studying the military defense of France's northeastern frontier. His solution, a "line of fortifications" from which a counterthrust could be mounted, was assumed by many to be support for the static defense of the Maginot Line, then under consideration.

Between 1927 and 1931 de Gaulle returned to active duty, first as major in the occupation army at Trier, and then with the general staff of the French army at Beirut. In 1932, however, he became secretary of the Superior Council of National Defense, remaining for four years at the center of French military planning. During this time he published two books, *The Edge of the Sword (Le Fil de l'épée)* and *Toward a Career Army (Vers l'armée de métier)*. In the first, published in 1932, he described the "moral renaissance" that could be brought about in the French army by a "man of character" whose traits—passion for action, self-reliance, diversity of talent, reserve, cultivation of prestige—would make him the object of the conservative military hierarchy's envy until, when danger threatened, he would finally be handed "the difficult task, the main job, the decisive mission." Two years later, in *Toward a Career Army*, he pleaded that the defense of France's fragile northeastern frontier could be accomplished only by maintaining a professional force equipped with tanks and trained in rapid mobility; but his ideas were rejected by the army hierarchy and the general public. *Toward a Career Army* was a publishing flop.

The book does, however, pose our first major problem of interpretation of de Gaulle's career, for his supporters have always claimed that this book proved de Gaulle's prophetic insight into the nature of future warfare. Several specific claims have been made for de Gaulle as the theorist of tank warfare: that he was the originator, in France at least, of ideas of tank warfare; that the German Panzer generals read his book, applied his ideas, and defeated France in 1940 with armored columns designed on de Gaulle's plan; and that France could have defeated the Germans in 1940 if its army had been equipped with the six armored divisions de Gaulle had proposed.

Duncan Grinnell-Milne, in the first selection, accepts these statements uncritically, and indeed speaks of General Guderian as de Gaulle's disciple. Military historians, however, such as Henri Bernard, claim that de Gaulle's importance has been overrated; that the doctrine of tank warfare was originated by the English, notably General Fuller and Captain Liddell Hart, a decade before de Gaulle wrote; that he was preceded even in France by General d'Estienne; and that the German generals formed their first tank divisions before de Gaulle's book was read in Germany. Furthermore, they add, it is almost impossible to say whether adoption of de Gaulle's ideas could have saved France in 1940 because it is uncertain what use the French command would have made of them. Even de Gaulle's brief successes at Moncornet on May 17–20 and near Laon on May 26–30, 1940, which are used by Gaullist writers to reinforce the impression that de Gaulle was a military genius, are dismissed by German tank commanders like Mellenthin as typical of the way the French threw away their tanks in useless sorties. The theme of "de Gaulle the military genius" became, however, an essential part of the Gaullist *mystique;* for at the next stage of his career, de Gaulle needed its glamor to capture the imagination of the French people.

As the German armies advanced throughout northern France in June 1940, de Gaulle was brought into Paul Reynaud's cabinet as Under-Secretary of War, a position he held for only eleven days; for on returning from a mission to London on June 16, de Gaulle learned that Reynaud had resigned and that the new Premier, Pétain, wished to seek an armistice with the Germans. That night he decided to leave France to create a center of French resistance in London. He was received by Churchill on June 17 and offered the use of the facilities of the British Broadcasting Company. On June 18 he made his famous appeal: "I, General de Gaulle, at present in London, ask all those French officers and men who are now, or may be in the future, on British soil . . . all engineers and skilled workers . . . to get in contact with me. Whatever happens, the flame of French resistance must not go out, and shall not go out." On June 19 he declared that "the ordinary forms of power have disappeared. . . . I, General de Gaulle, French soldier and leader, feel that I am speaking in the name of France."

De Gaulle was henceforth "the man of June 18"; the decision to break with Pétain's regime was the turning point of his life. The second group of readings presents the controversy over this decision. In the strict legal sense, de Gaulle was deserting from the army and denouncing the constitutional government of France. He had, therefore, to appeal to a higher law than that by which Pétain was invested as Premier. The Gaullist argument, which by 1944 had been accepted by the vast majority of French people, is given in the excerpt from Georges Cattaui's biography, *Charles de Gaulle: The Man and His Destiny.* De Gaulle was not a deserter, because a soldier's duty is to continue the battle when his leaders fail; he was not a traitor, because the honor of France had to be saved. But the Gaullist claim goes much further —that at the moment of his decision he incarnated France, or, as de Gaulle remarked, "j'étais la France."

Some of the awkward consequences of this claim are pointed out by one of de Gaulle's most persistent critics, Alfred Fabre-Luce, who argues that de Gaulle never recovered from the need to prove that treason can become legitimacy. English historian David Thomson argues, however, that de Gaulle realized the revolutionary character of his break with Pétain and chose to base his power on the Jacobin theory of the "general will," espousing as corollary the need for a complete renovation of French society. For Thomson, de Gaulle became not a Joan of Arc but a Maximilien Robespierre. A further difficulty of de Gaulle's lack of any legal mandate became clear in 1940 when the United States government decided to maintain diplomatic relations with Vichy and to ignore the Free French so far as possible, and again in 1942 when President Roosevelt decided that he preferred to deal with an apolitical soldier like General Giraud rather than with a self-appointed government like de Gaulle's. The acrid relationship between Roosevelt and de Gaulle during the war years was due not merely to a clash of temperaments, which certainly existed, but to Roosevelt's refusal to believe that de Gaulle was the incarnation of France and, perhaps even more, to his belief that France ought no longer to be treated as a great power. Many writers have taken sides in this quarrel, accusing Roosevelt of short-sightedness or de Gaulle of intransigence. Arthur Layton Funk makes no case for Roosevelt or de Gaulle but sees in their relationship the character of a Euripidean tragedy, in which men of fixed opinions move into inevitable conflict, with effects baneful to both.

By the time of the D-Day invasion of France, de Gaulle had given his French Committee of National Liberation (Comité Français de Libération Nationale, CFLN) the form of a future government of France; he had created under his own control an army of 250,000 men, and been recognized as its head by the Resistance in France. As the Allied armies liberated northern France, the popular support de Gaulle enjoyed was obvious, and the CFLN, now remodeled as the Provisional Government of the French Republic, won *de facto* recognition by the Allies. On August 25, acclaimed by a crowd of some two million, de Gaulle strode triumphantly down the Champs Elysées from the Arc de Triomphe to the Place de la Concorde, ending the day of apotheosis with a *Te Deum* in the cathedral of Notre Dame. For the next eighteen months he continued to govern France, working through a coalition of Communists, Socialists, and Christian Democrats, which restored order, carried out a purge of wartime collaborators, and nationalized several key industries. De Gaulle sought to restore France's great power positions by winning a share in the invasion and occupation of Germany, signing a treaty of friendship with Russia, and taking a place for France in the Council of Foreign Ministers. However, when the political parties prepared a constitution for the Fourth Republic which seemed to de Gaulle to perpetuate the governmental weakness of the Third, he startled and annoyed the French people by suddenly resigning the premiership on January 20, 1946, and going into self-imposed exile. De Gaulle's initial sortie into politics, the first "Gaullism," thus ended on a sour note.

The constitution of which de Gaulle disapproved was ratified in October 1946, although by a vote of only 35 percent of the eligible electors, and, as de Gaulle had warned, a series of unstable governments proved ineffective in dealing with France's worsening economic troubles, its social conflicts, and its colonial problems. On April 7, 1947, at Strasbourg, de Gaulle called for the formation of a Rally of the French People, a vast popular movement that would, he hoped, sweep him back into power.

This second Gaullism, which is the subject of the third group of readings, was to prove even more controversial than the first. The RPF claimed to reunite the French nation, which the political parties were fragmenting, in support of a leader who had previously saved the country in its hour of danger; it denounced the Communists as separatists; and, to its leader's disappointment, it drew its support largely from political conservatives. The failure of the RPF is attributed by French political scientist François Goguel to its transformation into a political party like the others as a result of its own inability to work with the center parties, which still resented de Gaulle's method of governing in 1944–1946. To many of its opponents, however, the second Gaullism bore all the marks of a new fascist party, a conclusion that is endorsed in a very qualified manner by H. Stuart Hughes and vigorously opposed by the well-known French philosopher, sociologist, and journalist Raymond Aron. The question whether the RPF was a fascist movement ceased to have reality when the elections of 1951 proved that the nation had not rallied to de Gaulle. His own supporters fell away, some accepting office—they lined up for soup, de Gaulle explained contemptuously while the remaining faithful, by their consistent obstruction in parliament, gave Gaullism a reputation for intransigent conservatism.

After 1955 de Gaulle deliberately disassociated himself from his followers, rarely appearing in public and devoting himself in the isolation of his country home at Colombey-les-deux-Eglises to writing his war memoirs. "In the tumult of men and events," he wrote, in what might have been a poignant envoi to his political career, "solitude was my temptation. Now, it was my friend. With whom else can one be contented when one has met History?" Yet at the same time, he returned to the theme of that legitimacy which only he could represent and which "would be imposed, by general consent, as soon as the country would run the risk of once again being torn apart and threatened." Crisis in Algeria provided that danger. On May 28, 1958, President René Coty informed the National Assembly that "in the peril of the country and of the Republic," he had asked "the most illustrious of Frenchmen" to form a government. De Gaulle was invested by the National Assembly as Premier on June 1, by a vote of 329 to 224, and given power to govern by decree for six months and to prepare a new constitution for popular ratification.

The fourth group of readings deals with three of the most debated aspects of the third Gaullism: the circumstances of de Gaulle's return to power; his treatment of the Algerian problem; and his foreign policy, with particular emphasis on his blocking of British membership in the Common Market.

The reasons for the successful appearance of the third Gaullism are still disputed. The tangled plots in Algeria and France, which were manipulated by Gaullist leaders to make de Gaulle appear the only alternative to civil war, are skillfully unwoven by two British political scientists, Philip M. Williams and Martin Harrison. Although they conclude that de Gaulle was not personally involved in the events in Algeria, their account of the influence these events had on the politicians in Paris and of de Gaulle's use of the danger inherent in the situation in Algeria to win power on his own terms force one to ask whether his insistence on legal investiture was anything more than a mockery. Was the German Socialist newspaper *Vorwärts* correct in concluding: "General de Gaulle did not take power legally. A parliament that submits to blackmail under the threat of civil war by factious generals and a government that assures these same generals of its confidence instead of dismissing them immediately from their command and bringing them before a court-martial cannot now use the excuse that the election of de Gaulle as Premier followed regular parliamentary and democratic procedures." The Gaullist answer, given in an excerpt by the senator Léo Hamon, a "Gaullist of the Left," is that a spontaneous "crystallization" around de Gaulle took place when France was in danger, because amid the decadence of the Fourth Republic, he still represented the French nation's longing for greatness and national unity. The "Algiers coup" of May 13, for Hamon, is a side issue.

De Gaulle's primary task on his return to power was to bring an end to the costly and bloody war in Algeria. Yet it took him four years before he reached agreement with the leaders of the Algerian rebels on a cease-fire and peace settlement, and even then he gave the rebels almost everything they had entered the war to win. For some writers, de Gaulle's policy on the Algerian war is proof that he is, above all, a realist. Paul-Marie de la Gorce, a French journalist and historian of the French army, explains the long delay by pointing to the intransigence and internal difficulties of the rebel leaders in the National Liberation Front (Front de Libération Nationale, FLN), to the opposition of European civilians and a politicized army in Algeria, and to de Gaulle's "evolutionary and empirical" approach to the Algerian problem. Yet the evidence presented may be interpreted far less sympathetically. Need it have taken four years of further bloodshed to achieve a settlement on the FLN's own terms? English historian Dorothy Pickles asks. Did not the long delay cause the worsening of relations between the Europeans and Moslems in Algeria and between the French army and government that culminated in the outrages of the Secret Army Organization (Organisation de l'Armée Secrète, OAS), in Algeria and France and brought about the flight of almost the entire European population of Algeria?

It is de Gaulle's foreign policy, however, that has aroused the greatest passions, particularly since the end of the Algerian war in 1962. Before that time he had succeeded in quieting many of the fears expressed on his return to power. He had carried through a program of decolonization that had given independence to the French territories in Africa. He had accepted the obligations of membership in the Common Market (European Economic Community) and had even strengthened the Community by forcing the inclusion of agriculture. He had sought reconciliation with Germany, political union of the Six, and firmness toward Russia. In January 1963, however, without consulting any of France's Common Market partners, he used his press conference to announce his personal veto on British membership, and a week later he signed a bilateral treaty of friendship and cooperation with West Germany. These two events led to a vigorous reappraisal of de Gaulle's foreign policy throughout Europe and America. Was de Gaulle's nationalism a threat to European unification? Was his concept of a "Europe of the states" a return to seventeenth-century ideas of the balance of power? Was there a positive side to his policy? German federalist leaders Ernst Friedlaender and Katharina Focke express the bitterness of those Germans who had worked since 1945 to replace the national spirit in Germany with a higher loyalty to Europe. For them de Gaulle is an anachronism whose nationalism is alien to twentieth-century Europe. Writing in the influential British journal *International Affairs* just three months after the veto, French political scientist and foreign policy expert Alfred Grosser calls for an "emotional truce" in considering de Gaulle's foreign policy. Many aspects of de Gaulle's policy, he points out, are positive and far-sighted.

The final group of readings presents several answers to a question seemingly asked by everyone: What is de Gaulle really like? Emmanuel d'Astier, a Resistance leader who frequently saw de Gaulle during the war years, provides a classic sketch of a historical figure who feels only contempt for his fellow men, a "great, cold prelate whose kingdom is France." The key to de Gaulle, d'Astier feels, lies in "those few days at the end of June and beginning of July, 1940, during which he incarnated France"; but d'Astier did not know him then. Nora Beloff, a British journalist passionately disappointed at de Gaulle's rejection of British membership in the Common Market, says that de Gaulle "invented his own character," so no one will ever know what the real man is like. She does, nevertheless, give her own unflattering analysis of his character. Another leading British journalist and historian, Alexander Werth, finds d'Astier's version exaggerated. Churchill, too, he thinks, failed to understand de Gaulle because they were both anachronisms. The explanation of de Gaulle, Werth concludes, is in *The Edge of the Sword*—the "man of character" whom de Gaulle describes is himself.

Perhaps there are several de Gaulles as there have been several Gaullisms. When a prominent society lady once remarked to de Gaulle apologetically that she had not always been a Gaullist, he replied, "Why, my dear lady, I have not always been one myself."

In the reprinted selections footnotes appearing in the original sources have in general been omitted unless they contribute to the argument or better understanding of the selection.

DUNCAN GRINNELL-MILNE (1896–   ) served as
air liaison officer with de Gaulle during the early
months of the Free French movement in London.
Turning to writing after a career in broadcasting and
business, he published a study of the Royal Navy in
1940, *The Silent Victory* (1958), and *The Triumph
of Integrity: A Portrait of Charles de Gaulle* (1961).
While the biography of de Gaulle has been criticized
by military historians for overrating de Gaulle's contribution as a military theorist, it illustrates the
admiration he has inspired among foreigners who have
known him personally and presents one of the main
arguments used in 1940 to justify his leadership of the
French Resistance—that he was a military genius
whose insight into the nature of the coming war had
been ignored by the conservative hierarchy of the
French army but adopted by the German Army.*

The Military Genius

The obvious is what most men see too
late and men of genius see too soon. De
Gaulle belonged to the second category.
He was not the first to perceive the immense changes in methods of warfare
brought about by the internal combus-
tion engine, any more than he was the
first to appreciate the growing importance of the tank. But he was among the
first—others included, for France, General d'Estienne and, for Britain, General
Fuller and Captain Liddell Hart—to
grasp the idea of using a large force of
tanks (and other arms) independently of
the infantry which hitherto they had
been employed only to support; a force
of armour to be regarded not so much
as cavalry, but rather as it might be a

squadron of warships with auxiliaries,
compact, self-supporting, under its own
commander. He was certainly the first
in France to develop the idea in detail,
to lay down the composition of the unit,
the "armoured division," to prescribe its
organization, and then to examine its
purpose and vast strategic possibilities in
modern war. In this examination, and
in the logical conclusions he drew from
it, he led the world.

From prolonged study[1] he deduced,
for France, a basic figure of six
Armoured Divisions requiring for their
service 100,000 men. Since each unit
would include, as well as motor-cycle

[1] He published his conclusions in *Vers l' armée
de métier* (1934).—Ed.

* From Duncan Grinnell-Milne, *The Triumph of Integrity: A Portrait of Charles de Gaulle*
(London: The Bodley Head Ltd., 1961), pp. 61–65. Footnote omitted.

reconnaissance groups, tracked vehicles for infantry, motorized artillery and some five hundred tanks, it was evident that the men must be fully trained specialists, just as were the crews of warships or of aircraft, and that therefore the force as a whole was to be regarded as a small standing army ready for instant action on the outbreak of war. Since, moreover, the estimated fire-power of these six Armoured Divisions, supported of course by aircraft, would be superior to that of the entire French Army mobilized in 1914, a very large proportion of the mobilizable five millions would not be required as combatants; there would be a considerable saving in man-power and money, and the economy of the country in wartime would remain largely undisturbed. The provision of such a force, de Gaulle believed, might well deter the enemy from attacking at all; but in the event of war the conflict would be shorter and less costly, since he calculated that the spearhead thrust of the six Divisions would speedily be decisive.

From these calculations the conclusions were inescapable, and diametrically opposed. If war came, the Armoured force assisted by air power would smash through the enemy defences with the first hard blows, and would then proceed to an exploitation of the "breakthrough" far more devastating than anything contemplated in the previous War. Moving at 20–25 miles an hour, it would dislocate the enemy command, disrupt communications, paralyse troop formations; driving ever deeper into enemy country, it would occupy strategic points, isolate military centres and industrial areas; demoralization would follow swiftly and total collapse might well ensue. But the converse was also true: supposing that *not France, but the enemy* pos-

sessed this new weapon, the independent highly-specialized Armoured force, then at some time, at some point, under its assault supported by all arms even the strongest fortifications must be penetrated and the enemy Armour pour through to a similar and equally disastrous exploitation. The slow-moving masses of the French Army would be powerless to stop the drive–unless they could oppose it with an equally fast-moving force. The only answer to Armour, therefore, was Armour. The buckler of the north-eastern defences would be beaten down unless it held a spear.

In effect the design for the standing army of six Armoured Divisions, and the purpose for which they were intended, was an invention as revolutionary as the tank itself. But the inventor is seldom recognized in his own land, and the prophet is notoriously without honour. De Gaulle, after long reflection, began serious work on his project towards the end of 1932. By that time he was back in the office on the Boulevard des Invalides, to which he had returned after serving two years in command of the battalion on the Rhine and a further year on the staff of the commander-in-chief in Syria. In the interval he had also completed and published another book, *Le Fil de l'Epée,* in which he analysed the necessary characteristics of an ideal military commander. A profoundly penetrating work, it found favour in literary, but not in military circles where the author was now seen to be, worse than unorthodox, something of a disturbing influence, a nuisance who might be dangerous. He was given no encouragement in his new task.

The first news of the projected Armoured force was published in the authoritative "Political and Parliamentary

Review" in May 1933. It was warmly welcomed in political circles. A scheme that substituted 100,000 men for five millions, that gave increased security at diminished cost, that would satisfy the League's insistent advocacy of disarmament—and thereby rob Hitler of his principal argument in favour of rearming—such a scheme was exactly what was needed; it was brilliant common sense. At once the military hierarchy took fright. Reducing the mobilizable millions to a few hundred thousand would mean a reduction almost to zero of the cadres of officers; promotion would cease overnight; senior officers would be retired by the hundred. At all costs and without further consideration the scheme must be condemned. Rebuking de Gaulle, who was now looked upon as a trouble-maker with ideas above his station, the General Staff let it be known that under no circumstances would it tolerate any reorganization of the Army, that nothing need and nothing should interfere with the present super-excellent state of affairs. And the military chiefs, having turned de Gaulle down, turned themselves over and went to sleep. . . . The tumultuous events of 1934—the death of King Albert of the Belgians, and the subsequent renunciation by Belgium of the alliance with France; the

murder by Hitler of his opponents in Germany, the murder by his supporters of Chancellor Dollfuss in Vienna; the death of Hindenburg and the assumption of supreme power by the *Führer*—amid these sensational happenings one thing of greater consequence to the fate of Europe than all the rest passed almost unnoticed. Failing to impress the General Staff, de Gaulle tried to compel action by interesting the nation as a whole. His book, *Vers l'Armée de Métier,* was published in May. It was logical, convincing, concise. It cost about three shillings. It sold seven hundred and fifty copies; which is as good as saying that no one read it, outside of a few hostile critics and a handful of professional soldiers. The military attaché at the German Embassy bought some copies and sent them back across the Rhine; one of them was passed on to an energetic Colonel of Dutch extraction, by name of Guderian, whose theories of armoured warfare had been developing along much the same lines. With approval from on high, he got down to practical work. By 1935 the first *Panzer* Division was equipped and ready. It was, in every detail, a replica of de Gaulle's *Division Blindée*—alas, still on paper. Hitler's staff had marked well what Pétain had refused to read.

The claims that ideas of tank warfare originated with de Gaulle and that he influenced German tank commanders have been challenged by military historians. HENRI BERNARD (1900–) of the Royal Military School in Brussels, one of Belgium's foremost military historians, points out that German generals like Guderian, as well as de Gaulle himself, adopted the theories of tank warfare developed in England by such writers as Captain Sir Basil Henry Liddell Hart.*

The Truth on the Doctrine of the Use of Tanks

Since 1940, Charles de Gaulle has lived on the reputation of having been "the" precursor of the wise doctrine of the use of tanks, a doctrine adopted later by the Germans, assuring them their spectacular victories of 1939–1941. Out of respect for the man of June 18, I have always felt some scruple about giving the lie to this belief. I now feel that I ought to free myself of this scruple.

The brilliant officer of 1934 had, without any doubt, the merit of understanding the rational use of tanks in future warfare. It is regrettable that the great majority of Western military leaders should not have showed a similar foresightedness. But the ideas that de Gaulle expressed in *Vers l'armée de métier* were in no way his own individual ideas.

Others had proposed them before him.

In 1953 I had a long talk with General Guderian. I reminded him that certain Western authors had stated that the heads of the German armored forces had been inspired by de Gaulle. Guderian smiled and replied: "Those are certainly statements made after the event. For my part, I had never heard of de Gaulle before his appeal of June 18, 1940. Everything that we had learned on the question of tanks we owed to Fuller and Liddell Hart. Not to forget Percy Hobart and his experiments at Salisbury." And he added: "Nobody is a prophet in his own country. The Franco-British leaders did not wish to take up the ideas of their English precursors."

It was in May 1918, in fact, that

---

* From Henri Bernard, *"Le Général de Gaulle et la Belgique," Phare-Dimanche,* February 3, 1963. Translated by editor.

Colonel J. F. C. Fuller, head of the general staff of the Tank Corps, the man of Cambrai, made a long report to the Allied commander-in-chief proposing to him a breakthrough of the enemy front by an armored force of 5000 tanks: heavy tanks for the breakthrough, light tanks for its exploitation. His project was accepted for spring 1919. The armistice intervened.

In 1921 Fuller conceived of giant aircraft, carrying tanks, which would cross the seas to set tanks down on the invasion coasts.

In 1924 young B. H. Liddell Hart arrived on the scene. He set up the detailed organization of the future armored division. He proposed the combined action of tanks acting en masse and of support aircraft with bilateral radio contact. He conceived as well the autonomous tank army which would operate strategically to break the enemy communications and the vital arteries of his supplies "in the manner of Sherman."

De Gaulle, when he published *Vers l'armée de métier,* knew the papers of Liddell Hart. The organization of the armored division and tank army which he presents is like a twin sister to that of the British military writer. But I have sought in vain in his work for a single reference, a single back page note, that would give his sources. Neither Fuller, nor Liddell Hart, nor even General Estienne, who was a true French precursor, are cited.

This little fact is, in reality, a very small thing in the history of that period. It would not be worth the mention if knowledge of it did not contribute to a better understanding of the character of General de Gaulle and of his attitude today: this great man is sincerely, profoundly convinced that, in every circumstance, he alone has the predestined ability to grasp and to make known the Truth. . . .

Perhaps the most crucial event in de Gaulle's life was his decision to deny the legality of the government of Marshal Pétain and proclaim himself the center of continuing French resistance to the Germans, as he did in his radio speech from London on June 18. A court-martial in Clermont-Ferrand on August 2, 1940 gave one interpretation of his action by condemning him to death as a traitor and a deserter. GEORGES CATTAUI (1896–   ), who was long reputed to be de Gaulle's favorite biographer, gives the Gaullist interpretation of the action which, he claims, saved the honor of France. The hyperbolical style of this extract is typical of many of the early biographies that helped further the Gaullist Legend.*

► ||| *The Man of June 18*

De Gaulle refused to accept the surrender. *France has lost a battle,* he thought, and soon would add, *but she has not lost the war.* He did not believe the defeat definitive. At the height of the catastrophe, he retained his clarity of thought. He did not bow before the display of enemy strength. France must go on living; she must be defended. Among "the second-rate rulers," who see only the present moment, this stable man took the bridge of the imperiled ship. *He listened,* Péguy would say, *to the immense silence of his race.* He realized that one single act of betrayal stains a whole people. With the Nazis victorious, it would mean France enslaved for generations. Worse yet: the French spirit would be perverted, de-stroyed. If, in the decision of Charles de Gaulle, there was sudden insight, the ground was well prepared: he was the man of matured actions and sudden choices.

During that night of June 15–16 at Bordeaux, de Gaulle could not sleep. A long night of anguish, when everything was thought through, weighed. Leave France? Appear as a deserter, a dissident, a rebel? He perceived everything he would have to endure: the contempt of some, the hatred of others, slander, abuse . . . He saw with foreboding the lamentable fate of the banished and the refugee: exile, quarrels, the foreigner's handouts . . . He would have to leave everything, his country, his soldiers, his mother—whom he would

* From Georges Cattaui, *Charles de Gaulle: L'Homme et son destin* (Paris: Librairie Arthème Fayard, 1960), pp. 93–97, 101–103. Footnotes omitted. Translated by editor.

not see again (for she would pass away at Paimpont, in Brittany, far from her son but confident of his destiny).

De Gaulle was nearly fifty. He was at the crossroads. In that irrevocable moment, he felt himself living in the past, the present, and the future of that France whose History he was taking upon himself. He pondered. At dawn his decision was made. To the temptation to remain, to acquiesce, he said, *No*. To sacrifice, he said, *Yes*. He gambled on continued struggle. Everything was saved by a triple act of faith: trust in the endurance of Great Britain beneath the bombs of the enemy; foresight that the ambitions of Hitler would provoke the entry into the war of the United States and of Russia; above all, belief that the people of France would not accept slavery and, under the German yoke, would rise again to end the war in victory. Perhaps he remembered as well the prophetic words of his uncle, the Celtic scholar Charles de Gaulle, proclaiming that every soldier has the duty and the right to pick up the banner abandoned by faltering leaders. Going beyond conformity with a false code of discipline to obey only the voice of his conscience, the call of his French instinct alone, de Gaulle prepared to become a symbol of disobedience, a scandalous example. He would not be proved wrong. Tearing himself away from his native soil, on that morning of June 17 at 8:30, accompanied by Geoffrey de Courcel, he set flight into exile from the airport of Mérignac at Bordeaux. It was the honor of France that, in Churchill's phrase, de Gaulle carried with him in his small airplane. After a brief stop at Jersey—the island where the memory of another great exile lives on—de Gaulle landed in England.

He left, not unsure of the destiny of his country and himself, but confident in the justice of the cause to which he was sacrificing the present. If it were necessary for him, as for the Prussian Stein earlier, he would seek the freedom of his country at the ends of the earth. That day, in a momentary lightning flash, de Gaulle carried out the timeless achievement. And the "tremendous shaping of destiny" was fulfilled. Invested as a hero, he would be worthy of that investiture. He was going to live his legend.

There are times, someone has said, when freedom bears the name of one man. On June 18, 1940, the freedom of France bore this single name: *de Gaulle*. For fifty-two months, for the majority of French people one general would be only a name and a voice. That voice of June 18 spoke the only language compatible with honor. It took possession of History.

How can one evoke without emotion the extent of the impact, of the decisive involvement, that brought the Resistance into being? De Gaulle was then that event and made History. He was the voice of that people which says No, which chooses to fight. Thanks to him, if there was defeat, there was not total surrender, there was not betrayal: the true France continued. "Something has occurred," said the philosopher (Bergson), "something which might not have been, which would not have been, without certain circumstances, without certain men, without a certain man, perhaps."

Can one think of what the future would have been if, that day, this man had not been present, if he had not assumed the risk of responsibility for our salvation? Everything was not lost from then on because, through him alone, honor was safe.

Few men have known a more flagrant eruption of glory into their destiny. By one word, by one choice, by one act, this man, yesterday unknown, became illustrious: he became forever the man of June 18. And without doubt this fine title would be sufficient for the glory of someone else; but for him it was only "the first step in his journey"; he could not remain the man of one day, however great that day may have been when, by the words of one man, all were washed clean of shame. . . .

Formed in the veneration of the army, for a time a close associate of Marshal Pétain, his commander and his example, de Gaulle could only confront his old captain with a deep sorrow; but he owed himself first to France, which he saw bamboozled, which he thought misunderstood. He who alone had meditated for ten years on the need for the renovation of French arms; he alone who had foreseen the circumstances and the causes of the catastrophe; he alone who had suggested the methods for avoiding the disaster and assuring success; he whom no army leader was willing to support, why should he not stand forward and say openly what his soldier's, patriot's, and free man's conscience dictated?

Pétain, grown old, believed that his presence alone would deaden the shock between occupier and occupied; he believed that the virtue of his prestige alone would win concessions from the enemy. What he did not understand was that by putting up a screen he prevented the true reflexes from showing— and that to the great moral detriment of France. He thus disturbed people's consciences, he divided the nation. Not

understanding the true stake in the battle, the significance of the principles at issue, the utterly inhuman character of the enemy that France had to face, Pétain, Laval, and Darlan were going to maneuver. . . . Faced with this betrayal, de Gaulle exclaimed in his appeal of June 18:

Certainly we have been, we are overwhelmed by mechanized forces of the enemy, on land and in the air. Infinitely more than their numbers, it is the tanks, the planes, the tactics of the Germans that have made us pull back. But has the last word been said? Must hope disappear? Is the defeat definitive? No! believe me. . . . Nothing is lost for France. The same means that have defeated us can one day bring victory. For France is not alone. She has a vast empire behind her. She can unite with the British empire that holds the sea and is continuing the struggle. She can, like England, make endless use of the immense industry of the United States. This war is not settled by the battle of France. This war is a world war. All the errors, all the delays, all the suffering do not prevent there being in the world the necessary means for crushing our enemies one day. Battered today by mechanized force, we shall be able to conquer in the future by a superior mechanized force. The destiny of the world lies in that.

Whatever happens, the flame of French resistance must not go out and shall not go out.

At the appeal of that voice the sentiments hidden in the depth of bruised hearts awakened. One day Claudel would write in the name of France, "There is now someone who is myself standing upright and whom I hear speaking in my own voice."

ALFRED FABRE-LUCE (1899–   ), a well-known
French novelist, playwright, and publicist, intended
The Most Illustrious of Frenchmen (1960) to be "the
first critical biography of General de Gaulle." In
dealing with the events of June 18, 1940, Fabre-Luce
challenges claims such as that of Cattaui, that
de Gaulle's action brought the French Resistance into
being and saved France's honor, and argues that
de Gaulle, by legalizing an act of rebellion, created
for himself a lasting problem of establishing the
legitimacy of his government and the illegality of
future acts of insurrection.*

► *The Rebel*

When one cannot erase one's errors, one
deifies them.—Chateaubriand

In June 1940 Gaulle[1] decided not to
capitulate under any circumstances. One
could even say that this was a decision
he had always known within himself.
Would he be a protester in retirement?
A general who vainly fought a last
skirmish for honor alone on his home
ground? No. He was going to play his
own personal game at the highest political level. Two requests from others
encouraged him to do so: Mandel, the
Minister of the Interior, begged him not
to resign; General Spears, on Churchill's

orders, invited him to set up quarters in
London. In Bordeaux, where he spent
June 16, he feared arrest, as if his decision were visible on his face. He met
Spears in the British ambassador's hotel
room, went there by a roundabout way,
asked to spend the night on a British
cruiser anchored in the Gironde, and
the next day, after concealing his intentions, at the last moment boarded
Spears's plane which was returning to
London. On June 18, speaking on the
BBC in full uniform with white gloves,
he told the French that they had "the
absolute duty to continue to resist . . ."

The next day, June 19, in a second
speech, he made his message more precise: "In the name of France, I declare

[1] Fabre-Luce deliberately omits the "de" from
de Gaulle, on the ground that he is not of noble
birth.—Ed.

* From Alfred Fabre-Luce, *Le Plus illustre des Français* (Paris: René Julliard, 1960), pp. 71–75,
86–88. Footnotes omitted. Translated by editor.

formally what follows. Every French-man who still bears arms has the absolute duty to continue to resist." And he specified: "At the present time, I am speaking especially for French North Africa. . . ." The execution of this order would have brought about disastrous consequences. That did not lessen, as Moulin de la Barthète (director of Marshal Pétain's staff at the time) wrote, "its incomparable aesthetic value. . . ."

On the announcement of the armistice, two commentaries, accompanied by rival *Marseillaises,* confronted each other on the radio waves: "Our honor is safe. No one will use our planes and our fleet," said the quivering voice of Marshal Pétain. "Our fleet, our planes, our tanks, our arms, are to be delivered intact, so that the enemy may use them against our own allies," retorted the aggressive voice of Gaulle. It was the Marshal who was correct. But the *Marseillaise* of the General had the more authentic sound.

Few Frenchmen heard him. It appeared later as though the speeches of Gaulle got the Resistance movement started. That is an *a posteriori* impression. One of the leaders of the Resistance, Henri Frenay, wrote: "There is not one Frenchman in a thousand who heard the appeal of June 18 on the radio. There are scarcely more who knew him six months later." One of the rare parliamentary opponents of Pétain, Senator Révillon, who kept a diary at the time, does not even mention the appeal of the General. On the other side of the Channel, that appeal exerted little influence. On June 27 Churchill had to give up the hope that Gaulle would be able to harangue, with any chance of success, the French units stationed in Great Britain.

Behind his mask of resolution and imperturbability, Gaulle certainly went through a moral crisis. "As the irrevocable words flew away, I felt within myself a life coming to an end, that which I had led in the framework of a solid France and of an indivisible army. At forty-nine, I was beginning a hazardous adventure." No other general imitated his gesture. Gaulle alone broke with military discipline. Later he tried to close the door of disobedience behind him. When Giraud refused to accept from his hands the post of Inspector-General of the Army, he had General Chambe tell him: "No matter how high one is, one obeys the government. Without that, where would one end up?" The problem would appear again: in 1945 in Syria; in 1960 in Algiers. Gaulle had created, for himself as for his rivals and successors, a dangerous precedent....

From these years of uncertainty dated a legitimacy complex that would haunt Gaulle during the rest of his existence. In 1960, faced with the Algiers insurrection, he declared: "The legitimacy that I have embodied for twenty years. . . ." If one took this declaration literally, it would be necessary to conclude that between 1946 and 1958 the acts of the governments of a Fourth Republic of which he disapproved had only a dubious validity. René Coty himself, who gave up his position to him, would not have been a legitimate president, or rather would only have become it, for and by this act.

From the start, this theory contained in germ the radical purge of the Liberation. If the appeal of June 18 really sufficed to transfer legitimacy to London, all those who, after that date, recognized it as being in France, would have to be punished. That is why, by retroactive legislation, all the members of the governments formed by Pétain were automatically inculpated. If one accepts the premise, this conclusion is of impeccable logic. The difficulty is accepting it. Even in an emergency regime, even after a purge of the magistrature, Charles de Gaulle did not succeed in forcing it on the law courts.

Recalling in his memoirs the public trials before the High Court in 1945, he wrote: "What seemed to me essential in the indictment was less so in the eyes of many. For me, the capital fault of Pétain and his government was to have concluded the so-called 'armistice,' with the enemy, in the name of France. . . . And so I was annoyed to see the High Court, the parliamentary circles, the newspapers, refraining from criticizing the 'armistice' and, on the contrary, seizing at length upon facts that were only incidental to it." In fact, during the Pétain trial, the prosecutor, Mornet, who was hardly guilty of indifference, declared: "The armistice does not constitute one of the main points of the indictment . . . The process of treason begins from July 11, 1940." A disquieting remark, for if on July 11, 1940, Marshall Pétain had not yet committed treason, what was the situation, between June 18 and July 11, of Brigadier-General Charles de Gaulle who had rebelled against him? At the height of his triumph, the 1945 president felt himself becoming a victim of the purge he himself had decided upon.

He showed at moments that he knew the truth. He said to Rémy: "Charles VII and Joan of Arc did not have to reconstruct the State starting from nothing. Charles VII retained legitimacy." And to Queuille: "Mr. Minister of State, do you realize that you are a member of a revolutionary government?" As Jeanneney, President of the Senate in 1940, was being reproached for having allowed the armistice to be made, he replied: "Things were not so clear at that moment." These statements did not interrupt the unfolding of a system based upon the contrary assumption. But it was impossible in the end to make the French people as a whole accept the linking of legitimacy-treason that is the spiritual basis of Gaullism. Even François Mauriac, a Gaullist with fervent vocation, if not from the beginning, agreed: "The evidence, which proves the legality of the Vichy government, has been rejected."

DAVID THOMSON (1912–   ), Master of Sidney
Sussex College, Cambridge, is author of many books
on recent British and French History, including
The Democratic Ideal in France and England and
Democracy in France. In this selection from his short
study, *Two Frenchmen: Pierre Laval and Charles
de Gaulle* (1951), he argues that de Gaulle evolved
into a realistic politician who recognized the
revolutionary nature of his break with Vichy and
its corollary, the need to carry out a revolutionary
overhaul of French society.*

A Revolutionary Jacobin

The story of the relations between
General de Gaulle and General Giraud
is a new phase in the evolution both of
the French National Committee[1] and of
de Gaulle himself as a political leader.
During the perplexing weeks between
the emergence of Darlan[2] in North
Africa and his assassination [November
10–December 24, 1942], Giraud[3] as mili-

[1] The central organ of the Free French movement from September 1941 to June 1943.—Ed.

[2] Admiral Darlan, Commander-in-Chief of the
Vichy military forces, was given administrative
control of French North Africa after the Anglo-
American invasion of November 1942, in return
for ordering a cease-fire. He was assassinated on
December 24, 1942.—Ed.

[3] Giraud became de Gaulle's principal rival
when he was chosen High Commissioner of
French North Africa by the Imperial Council,
a Vichyite body whose decision was endorsed by
Roosevelt.—Ed.

tary chief kept repeating to journalists,
"I am a soldier. I will have nothing to
do with politics." De Gaulle, by now,
was adopting the view that "there is no
war without politics." From his experience of heading the Free French, he had
drawn this lesson: Giraud, some six
months out of his prison, had not. He
began by taking the politically absurd
view that, for the time, everybody was
to remain in their place: "political
prisoners in prison, Gaullists in London,
and Vichyites in power," as Renée Pierre-
Gosset pungently puts it. He was determined not to lead a revolutionary
movement, and wanted to do nothing
which might impede or complicate military operations. Gaullism, by now, had
acquired all the qualities of a restlessly

---

* From David Thomson, *Two Frenchmen: Pierre Laval and Charles de Gaulle* (London: The
Cresset Press, 1961), pp. 192–201. Footnotes omitted.

revolutionary movement, and as this is the essential clue to all that happened afterwards it is important to understand how this remarkable change had come about.

Charles de Gaulle's original act of defiance, in June, 1940, was of course in itself a revolutionary act. But it was some considerable time before the implications of it, as involving logically and inevitably a programme of revolutionary overhaul in France itself, came to be appreciated even by de Gaulle himself. Professor Brogan put the point clearly a few months after the North African landings [of November 8, 1942] when he wrote: "Without any planning, the de Gaulle movement became the chief, not the only but the chief, symbol of the under-privileged, the people of France, the people Admiral Leahy and Robert Murphy[4] did not meet. It may not have deserved to be the chief symbol; it is not and never has been the only symbol. Its role was threatened when Hitler invaded Russia. With all European peoples (including the English) the Russian resistance has been the great, heroic theme of this war. But the effect in France was to help the resistance movement, that is, to help de Gaulle. The Germans aided by shooting people indiscriminately as Communists or de Gaullists. Often their victims were neither. But the identification stuck. The Russians were the people who knew the answers concealed from Gamelin, Weygand and Pétain. The de Gaullists were the people who had never spoken well of the Germans, unlike MM. Pétain, Darlan and Laval. . . . Jacobinism, that is, revolutionary patriotism, was forced on the de Gaullist movement, especially after the beginning of the Russian war." In his speech in the Albert Hall to a rally of French

people on Armistice Day, 1942, de Gaulle chose to strike the authentic note of revolutionary Jacobinism, showing that he had at least by now appreciated the new role of his movement. "France knows, too, the cost of a regime whose social and moral fibres had hardened, so that the country first suffered from the indifference of the exploited masses and was then betrayed by coalitions of trusts and men in power. She means to establish at home a social and moral system in which each individual can live in dignity and security, and where no monopoly can exploit him or in any way obstruct the general interests." He spoke of setting up a "new democracy in which the sovereignty of the people may be fully exercised by election and control."

The prolonged contest between de Gaulle and Giraud for leadership of the French National Committee accentuated this transformation of what had been initially a pure resistance organization into a political movement. Compared with the non-political Giraud, de Gaulle emerged as an astute politician. His movement gradually transformed itself from a non-party into something of an all-party movement. Springing originally from his personal enterprise, it had grown meantime by accretion from the ranks of all who were most opposed to *capitulards*[5] and *attentistes*[6] alike. It remained, by process of natural selection, a band of men and women resolute and unwilling to compromise. But inclusion in its higher ranks of men who represented party-groupings on the underground front in France, or who had been closely associated with the parties of the Third Republic, gave it a different inner composition. It could fall, internally, into more politically recognizable strata

---

[4] The American representatives in Vichy.—Ed.

[5] Supporters of the armistice of 1940.—Ed.
[6] Advocates of a wait-and-see policy.—Ed.

once men like M. André Philip a Socialist, M. Georges Bidault a Catholic Democrat, and M. Louis Marin of the Right
became eminent among its leaders. It
also gave Gaullism the claim to more
organic connection and more systematic
contact with public opinion inside
France; which gave it a new basis of
authority and a stronger title to be representative of the French people than it
had had before, or than the ex-Vichy authorities ranged behind Giraud could
ever pretend to have. General Giraud's
position, being inherently ambiguous
and anomalous, could not indefinitely
withstand the claims of such a movement, for it had none of the Resistance
dynamism.

Giraud's authority rested on a somewhat fictitious apostolic succession of
credentials from Pétain via Darlan. It
sufficed to salve the consciences of the
conservatively minded military and naval
officers, civil servants and colonial ad-
ministrators who found any transference
of allegiance acutely embarrassing and
perplexing. But it could not grow. It
was Darlan, claiming to act on behalf of
Pétain, who had first appointed Giraud
as Commander-in-Chief; it was the Imperial Council, set up by Darlan and
composed of Pétain's nominees as Gov-
ernors-General, which on Darlan's death
appointed Giraud High Commissioner
for North Africa. The assumption un-
derlying his position was endorsement of
the legitimacy of Darlan's authority; its
consequence was association with ex-
Vichy officials. Both were absolutely
repudiated by Gaullism. For a time in
the winter of 1942 it looked as if France
was to have two leaders, de Gaulle in
London supported by Great Britain, and
Giraud in North Africa supported by
the United States. It was arranged that
they should meet at Casablanca, and the

world was presented with a carefully
arranged photograph of them stiffly
shaking hands.

At last a new French Committe of
National Liberation was set up in June,
1943. The great weakness of this Algiers
Committee was its consistent duality. It
had, at first, both Generals as Presidents,
and they were to preside alternately. Its
membership was equally mixed. Giraud,
whilst still protesting that he was no
politician, in fact held the authoritarian
conservative views which are normal to
service-chiefs who regard themselves as
"non-political." At first, too, both were
Commanders-in-Chief. But once a mer-
ger of the two bodies had been achieved
it was virtually inevitable that de Gaulle
should triumph, that the more dynamic
and revolutionary of the two wings of
the Committee should, in a revolutionary situation, take the lead. Giraud was
steadily and firmly ousted from political
power, and relegated first to a purely
military position and eventually to even
a subordinate military capacity, with de
Gaulle in supreme charge of both the
political and military direction of the
Committee. In November, 1943, a number of leaders of the resistance movements were included in the Committee.
The Consultative Assembly was set up,
and half its members represented the
resistance movements inside France. In
April, 1944, Giraud at last retired completely into private life, never to return.
(He died in March, 1949.) In the Consultative Assembly the rank and file of
the two movements got to know each
other, learned to work together for the
liberation of France, and the wounds
caused by the events of November and
December, 1942, were gradually healed.
But it is noteworthy that it took some
eighteen months, during which the resistance movements had to undertake

the tremendous task of planning French participation in liberation, before the wounds were healed: eighteen months which might have been more profitably and economically spent by French leaders than in such prolonged jostling of each other. The "temporary expedient" which saved British and American lives did so at the expense of French energies and self-respect. The de Gaulle who emerged from this phase was a more wily, astute and experienced politician than the de Gaulle of London. His eviction of Giraud from power was a masterpiece of machiavellian tactics. In Algiers he underwent his apprenticeship in parliamentary and governmental techniques. It was a subtle and insidious school.

By the end of 1943, therefore, the National Committee had found some homogeneity and unity; it had reinforced its authority through the institution of the Consultative Assembly; it had been officially recognized by the rest of the United Nations.[7] Under its rule in North Africa trade unions revived, Vichy laws were repealed and Vichy supporters removed from office, the Communist Party was allowed to come into the open and publish its paper *Liberté*. The Committee soon became, both in claim and in substance if not in name, the Provisional Government of France, even before D-Day. General de Gaulle could declare, amidst the applause of the Consultative Assembly, that "the French Committee of National Liberation is in fact the government of the French Republic." It was at least a shadow-government, and it set about preparing to take over actual provisional administration of metropolitan France after liberation. That the new regime

should be in form parliamentary was made more probable by the authority won by the Consultative Assembly in Algiers. The Committee looked more and more to it to furnish that basis of moral authority and popular approval which it most needed. De Gaulle summed up the relationship between Committee and Assembly like this. "This support brings to it, first, greater national authority to justify and mobilize against enemies and traitors all the forces of the nation. This support allows it to have, in the concert of free peoples, greater authority and wider hearing for our service to the common cause. This support, finally, is overwhelming proof that democracy, to whose laws we have been faithful and which we are now restoring in practice, is identical with the highest interests of France." The Assembly, during the spring of 1944, established a degree of ascendancy and control over the Committee which was very inadequately suggested by its title of "Consultative" Assembly. It criticized policy, it passed resolutions, it insisted on inquiring into how far its "advice" had been taken, and in short behaved increasingly like a real parliament. Whilst Darnand and his collaborationist militias were forcing civil war in France, the Assembly clamoured for more thorough "purification" of the North African administrations, and criticized the inadequacy of the Committee's rather formal and legalistic outlook for the realities of a revolutionary situation. It was a case of the Jacobins ousting the *Feuillants*[8] all over again. But even the formidable immediate tasks did not prevent the laying of more long-range plans. The idea which later bore fruit as the French

---

[7] The coalition fighting against Germany, Italy, and Japan.—Ed.

[8] Constitutional monarchists during the French Revolution.—Ed.

Union was mooted in the early months of 1944 by M. Lapie in the Consultative Assembly. Individuals, too, like M. Vincent Auriol, won their future official eminence in the Fourth Republic by their activities in the preparatory debates in Algiers. Decisions, such as the extension of the vote to women, and the resolve to hold early general elections after liberation, were also reached long before the expulsion of the Germans from French soil. From the earliest stages in the genesis of the Fourth Republic it was General de Gaulle who presided over its creation. He, more than any other person, was the mid-wife of the Fourth French Republic.

Was this the attainment of that "new power" which de Gaulle had originally mentioned in October, 1940, in his broadcast from Brazzaville? It must be noted that the whole conception of a "Fourth Republic" was by no means new. In the years between the wars several proposals had been made for a revision of the Third Republic radical enough to justify its renumbering. Jean de Granvillers had urged a "Fourth Republic" with plebiscitary foundations; Marcel Déat and Jacques Doriot, both to become extreme collaborators of the Germans, had equally clamoured for a new more authoritarian and a less parliamentary "Fourth Republic." The very phrase, and the concepts of a revolutionary breach with the parliamentary traditions of the pre-war regime which it implied, thus had ill-omened associations. It may be sensible and natural to number monarchs, but it becomes slightly absurd to go on numbering Republics. Yet de Gaulle and his followers deliberately favoured this notion, presumably because it chimed with their essentially revolutionary impetus. The subsequent Gaullist *Rassemblement*

would, as some of its members have said, prefer a "Fifth Republic" to replace the Fourth.

Before considering his influence on the new Republic, it is necessary to notice the influence of the revolutionary situation on his own character and outlook. The course of events after 1940 forced all French leaders of resistance to go behind the forms of constitutionalism and the principles of the rule of law, and to seek authority from the fountainhead of French national will—popular sovereignty. They turned inevitably to traditionally Jacobin ideas of the "general will," as described by Jean-Jacques Rousseau and as transformed in practice by the French Revolution. They concluded that the "general will" of the French people exercised its "national sovereignty" directly through organized resistance to the German invader, and by proxy through loyalty to the cause of Gaullism and to the French National Committee. The Committee claimed to serve as temporary trustee for French interests internationally. It was less a matter of restoring democracy to France than of restoring France to democracy. This could be achieved only through a momentous act of national will, which would create a new political order. This moment had to be prepared for in Algiers by provisional plans and firm leadership. It all involved a theory not of parliamentary constitutionalism, not of the rule of law, not of direct continuity with republican legality and the Third Republic: it was essentially a theory of revolutionary Jacobinism. And it was a theory which General de Gaulle, both by reason of his position as the focus of Gaullist *mystique* and by his grasp of the actual situation, fully adopted and endorsed. He acted on the notion of an implicit mandate from the French people, and regarded it as his task to canalise this popular will through the Consultative Assembly, to provide a vehicle for it through the National Committee. He told the Consultative Assembly, on 27th March, 1944, "Some speakers have referred ... to the importance which the attitude and decisions of the Assembly and the Government might have abroad. The Government begs you to take account only of what emerges from the will of the nation, of that and nothing else." In his public speeches and pronouncements he increasingly adopted the vocabulary and jargon of the Jacobin demagogue, and there is not the slightest reason to doubt his sincerity in so doing. The Cross of Lorraine was now inscribed with the ideals of "Liberty, Equality, Fraternity"; Joan of Arc held hands with Maximilien Robespierre....

President Roosevelt refused to recognize de Gaulle's claim to sole political leadership of France either as the incarnation of France, as Cattaui describes him, or as representative of the "general will" of the French people, as in Thomson's analysis. While many historians have unabashedly taken sides in the Roosevelt–de Gaulle dispute, ARTHUR LAYTON FUNK (1914–   ), after a dispassionate examination of Franco-American relations during the "crucial years" of de Gaulle's career (1943–1944), finds that de Gaulle worsened relations by his lack of realism, but that Roosevelt must also share the blame for a conflict that damaged the Allied cause.*

De Gaulle and Roosevelt: A Euripidean Drama

One of the curious anomalies to emerge from World War II exists in the fact while Frenchmen deeply respect the name of Franklin D. Roosevelt and Americans enthusiastically honor Charles de Gaulle as France's great liberator, both Roosevelt and de Gaulle, holding tenaciously to diametrically opposed views about France, regarded each other with suspicion and mistrust. To President Roosevelt, France was a dismembered, defeated country, leaderless and and bankrupt, whose disposition must await the war's unpredictable end; for de Gaulle, she was a bewildered victim whose temporary deviation from the road of traditional grandeur could be corrected by placing her trust in the leader of Fighting France. When de Gaulle met the President for the first time in January, 1943, at the Casablanca Conference, he endeavored to persuade Roosevelt that he possessed the moral, if not the legal right, to represent the French people. Joan of Arc, he argued, had never received any more formal investment from the people than he to lead France against her enemies. But de Gaulle's vivid presentation of his case increased the President's hostility, and the analogy with St. Joan served only to provide anecdotal material which the President later employed skillfully in denigrating de Gaulle to hundreds of listeners. In his many retellings of the story, Roosevelt twisted de Gaulle's arguments to make them appear as if the General had arrogantly

* From *Charles de Gaulle: The Crucial Years, 1943–1944*, by Arthur Layton Funk. Copyright 1959 by the University of Oklahoma Press. Pages 3–4, 270–272, 295, 297–299, 301–303, 316–318. Footnotes omitted.

portrayed himself as a twentieth-century Maid of Orléans.

The interchange between de Gaulle and the President at Casablanca took place over two and one-half years after de Gaulle had dramatically flown from Bordeaux, armed only with his stubborn determination to bring France back into the war. Long before they met, each had solidified his thinking into a pattern which inevitably brought them into conflict—a conflict in which not only Americans and French were to be entangled, but in which British interests were so powerfully involved that dangerous strains were produced between French and British and between British and Americans. The story of relations between the Fighting French and the United States moves with the predestined tragic pace of Euripidean drama; once the positions had been assumed, every action, every chance occurrence, every speech pushed the protagonists into situations from which neither could extricate himself with ease or dignity. . . . Roosevelt's antipathy toward de Gaulle derived basically from four sources. These were:

First, his attitude toward France. In Roosevelt's judgment, France was an exhausted, defeatist, confused country which did not correspond to de Gaulle's perorations about historical glory and grandeur. Because of the few thousand Frenchmen who had left their homes to join him, de Gaulle had no right to speak on behalf of the forty million who appeared to be satisfied with Marshal Pétain. If, indeed, de Gaulle represented the French people, they should have the right to say so after the country was liberated, but de Gaulle should not meanwhile be given the "title deeds" to France. This aspect of his policy coincided with Roosevelt's habitual wartime insistence on postponing political de-

cisions until the peace conference and subordinating civil to military problems.

Second, his personal mistrust of de Gaulle. Although the President enjoyed mimicking de Gaulle's Joan of Arc attitude as he had encountered it at Casablanca, it is not likely that Roosevelt's mistrust derived solely from his brief interviews with the General in January, 1943. But he did not trust de Gaulle's judgment or his tactics. There was a long history: the difficulties following the Anglo-Free French invasion of Syria; the Gestapo methods of Colonel Passy's BCRA; the vindictive anti-American editorials in the Gaullist newspaper *La Marseillaise;* the violence of André Philip; the dictatorial attitudes, the exaggerated claims, and the prima donna-like demeanor of de Gaulle; the Giraud ouster; and the methods employed to obtain representation on the Italian Commission. Stimson wrote: "To the President, de Gaulle was a narrow-minded French zealot with too much ambition for his own good and some rather dubious views on democracy." As time went on, it would become more and more difficult for the President to reverse himself. Duff Cooper explained Roosevelt's stubborness in regard to de Gaulle by pointing out that the President had backed two losers, Darlan and Giraud, and was understandably reluctant to admit that he had been wrong all along. Such an about-face would come hard to the man who sometimes referred to himself as "a pigheaded Dutchman." In 1954 the present writer had the opportunity to ask de Gaulle how he interpreted the President's antagonism. De Gaulle commented on the difference between his and Roosevelt's concept of France and then went on to say: "Roosevelt was a star—*une vedette* —and he disliked sharing the spotlight. He had difficulties in getting along with anyone, like Churchill, for example, who was also a star, but whom Roosevelt did not like, although both made great pretense of friendship. With his physical handicap to overcome, Roosevelt was obsessed with a psychological requirement of rising above his difficulties, of being the principal in the show." De Gaulle made a point of insisting that he thought his personal relations with Roosevelt were extremely cordial; "But our policies were entirely different."

Third, his concept of the postwar world. Roosevelt believed that collective security, implemented by friendly accord among the great powers, would put an end to the international friction generated by balance of power, spheres of influence, and imperialism. He believed he would find in Stalin an ally to impose this concept on Churchill, but he was convinced that de Gaulle would place himself in the opposition. Roosevelt was not inclined to give power to a man who might stubbornly oppose postwar efforts of the United Nations to establish trusteeships over Indochina and other colonial areas.

Fourth, his employment of unsound premises and misinformation in formulating his French policy. Roosevelt was wrong in his belief that civil war would develop in France, wrong in thinking that de Gaulle would establish a dictatorship, and wrong in his estimate of de Gaulle's relationship to the "revolutionary" elements of the Resistance. When one realizes that Stimson and Eisenhower, and later Secretary Hull and Robert Murphy, favored co-operation with de Gaulle and when one takes cognizance of the fact that virtually all reputable newspapers, including the *New York Times,* opposed the President, it is difficult to understand how he could have insisted on his policy unless he had access to information not

generally known, on which he placed great reliance. It is not unlikely that intelligence from OSS and Psychological Warfare failed to reach or influence the President; on the other hand, reports from Admiral Leahy, from General Giraud, and from other sources may have convinced him that he possessed "inside" information unavailable at other levels. . . .

It is difficult to point out advantages in the policy which the President had so long and so obstinately pursued. A case can be made for nonacceptance of de Gaulle during 1940 and 1941, and it is even arguable that introduction of de Gaulle into North Africa at the time of the landings would have served no purpose; but a point had been reached toward the end of 1943 when further by-passing of de Gaulle and the FCNL operated against rather than for Allied interests. Particularly after January, 1944, when the State and War Departments concurred in a policy of recognition, did the President's intransigence become indefensible. His inaction resulted in lack of guidance and confusion among those whose task was to implement policy, and it led to a series of *de facto* arrangements which could have been brought about sooner and more easily with intelligent leadership at top levels.

As Churchill had long since pointed out, *recognition* is simply a word, and it has no meaning except in terms of practical results. Recognized or not, de Gaulle's government was coping day by day with France's internal problems; without recognition the Provisional government had been able to negotiate Lend-Lease agreements, arrange for arms' deliveries, regulate currency matters, and participate in some international conferences. Now the question uppermost in the minds of Frenchmen, who accepted the long-delayed recognition with complacency, was the extent to which it would mean entry into higher Allied councils. If France would have to persist in standing at the door outside the council chamber, obtaining news from the syndicated press, she might as well be unrecognized. As he had done a year earlier after the formulas resulting from the first Quebec Conference had been announced, de Gaulle waited, not without cynicism, to learn what "recognition" might really mean to his government. . . .

. . . Whatever material benefits the French may have obtained from their relations with the United States and the other Allies, de Gaulle never was able to achieve what he most earnestly desired, acceptance as a cobelligerent by the Big Three. Some years after the war, de Gaulle told a group of his adherents that France must never again sit on the edge of her chair when invited to Allied war councils. The obligation of receiving crumbs from the table, of being excluded from meaningful deliberations on strategy, and of not being trusted to receive vital information tremendously irritated de Gaulle and his colleagues. The French leaders were brought to Casablanca virtually under guard and were not even invited to Quebec, Cairo, Teheran, Yalta, Potsdam, or the sessions of the Combined Chiefs of Staff. Small comfort emerged from French participation at conferences like UNRRA, to which representatives of all the United Nations, large and small, had been invited. Even membership in the Italian Advisory Commission proved a shallow accomplishment when it became apparent that the Commission possessed no real influence in determining policy on Italian administration.

French exclusion from Big Three deliberations by no means resulted simply from Roosevelt's hostility to de Gaulle. No belligerent making a minor contribution in men and materials was invited to these discussions. All three chiefs of state agreed that the Big Three was a very exclusive club, the entrance fee being 5,000,000 soldiers or the equivalent. Because it was obvious that France, even with additional man power available after liberation, could not equip and train more than a minute fraction of that number before the end of the war, neither Churchill, Roosevelt, nor Stalin entertained the slightest thought of bringing France into their strategic conferences.

It cannot, of course, be denied, in reviewing Franco-American wartime relations, that a significant factor in determining the course of policy was the personal intervention and concern of the American President. But there were other factors as well. At the beginning of the war, regardless of the White House attitude, the strong State Department devotion to Vichy would probably have required a maintenance of relations with Marshal Pétain at least until December, 1941, when the United States entered the war. After Pearl Harbor, in the course of 1942, as recognition of the Vichy regime became less and less defensible, a vigorous Presidential decision to deviate sharply from the traditional attitude could easily have been made. There was no public pressure to hinder such a decision—on the contrary—and while effective support of de Gaulle might have irritated Cordell Hull, whose judgment, nettled by bitter memories of Saint Pierre and Miquelon,[1] fell short of impartiality, it must be recalled that General Donovan's OSS and members of the War Department recognized, even at that time, the significance and value of Fighting France to the war

[1] French islands off Newfoundland which were seized by the Free French on December 24, 1941, in spite of Roosevelt's guarantee to the Vichy representative that the status quo in the Western Hemisphere would not be disturbed.—Ed.

effort. That the Vichy policy prevailed, and that de Gaulle found the door unceremoniously shut in 1942, was in part the consequence of a series of fortuitous but related circumstances. If the Anglo-American decision to launch a cross-Channel offensive had not been subverted by the adoption of "Torch," the entire North African political fiasco might have been avoided. It is of course idle, however fascinating, to wonder whether, in the event that original plans for a Roosevelt–de Gaulle meeting in 1942 had been adhered to, the President might have developed a more favorable outlook toward the Free French. But once it had been decided to move into North Africa, where Robert Murphy's groundwork with anti-German, anti-Gaullist elements made a *rapprochement* with the Fighting French impossible, the break with de Gaulle became inevitable. To the extent that Roosevelt was personally responsible for the "Torch" decision he was responsible for an anti-de Gaulle attitude's becoming official United States policy. One could not work simultaneously with Darlan and de Gaulle; one could work simultaneously with Giraud and de Gaulle only with the greatest difficulty. All of Roosevelt's great gifts for compromising extremes and for exerting his personal charm to erase misunderstandings among subordinates failed in the face of a gap as unbridgeable as that which stretched between the dissidence of de Gaulle and the dissidence of Giraud. . . .

It is not so easy to exonerate Roosevelt of charges that his reluctance to recognize a de Gaulle-headed government was unrealistic and contrary to the best interests of the United States and the war effort. If exclusion of de Gaulle from North Africa was thrust upon the Allies by the nature of the invasion, acceptance of de Gaulle, once he had achieved domination of the French Com-

mittee of Liberation, was logical and inevitable. The question was not whether de Gaulle and the FCNL should be recognized but how soon—in other words, at what time did de Gaulle exercise such control over the Committee and over Resistance elements in France that failure to work with him produced disadvantages far outweighing the benefits? By October, 1943, there was good evidence that de Gaulle, not Giraud, was the man to work with; by December this evidence was conclusive; and by January, 1944, virtually every responsible officer in the North African theater and in Washington, including Eisenhower, Murphy, Wilson, McCloy, Stimson, and even Hull, had become convinced that closer relations with the FCNL were imperative. The responsibility for denying the Committee falls squarely on the shoulders of the President, who, for month after month—from January to July, 1944—stubbornly refused to submit. It can be pointed out that during these months Roosevelt's vitality was sapped by illness and that Harry Hopkins, also ill, was not available to provide the President with that sensible counsel which sometimes served to mitigate his chief's carelessness and obstinacy. But this defense can in no wise excuse the President for so centralizing control of foreign policy that in case of his disability no other agency could serve to reach necessary decisions.

To be sure, de Gaulle did nothing to make the President's task easier. Scarcely did American policy show signs of softening, when the General would initiate a crisis—over Corsica, Italy, the Mediterranean Commission, the Levant states, or Giraud—and act with such arrogance, refusing to descend from his Olympian heights, that serious misgivings were of necessity entertained in Washington about the possibility of working effectively with him. It may be that Roosevelt's offhand comments about the future of Morocco and Indochina, or his often-repeated statements on "local arrangements," were not calculated to calm Gaullist apprehensions; but power is accompanied by privilege, and de Gaulle as much as anyone had reason to be aware of that fact of political life. . . .

None of President Roosevelt's expressed fears about de Gaulle and the Free French materialized. It may be that Roosevelt opposed Free France because no proof could be adduced that de Gaulle was the French people's choice, it may be that he was lukewarm about de Gaulle because he believed he saw in him an opponent of collective security; or it may be that he was loath to furnish him his "white horse" because he distrusted and disliked him; but when it became clear that in spite of the President's personal opinion de Gaulle was to become the French chief of state, the better part of political wisdom should have dictated that Roosevelt could achieve his ends more successfully—as in the contest between the Sun and the Wind to make the Traveller remove his coat—by means more subtle than forceful antagonism. Roosevelt feared that de Gaulle would make himself a dictator, but de Gaulle, as he had promised, surrendered his powers to the first elected Assembly at the end of 1945; Roosevelt found de Gaulle unsympathetic to the trusteeship idea, but the original trusteeship concept never achieved fruition; Roosevelt feared civil war in France, but de Gaulle proved to be the best possible safeguard against internal disturbance; Roosevelt believed that other political leaders from inside France would emerge, but they did not. For a host of groundless fears the President interposed his solitary but powerful opposition to a policy which would have been, as events proved, in the American interest; and for the first half of 1944 no positive action in regard

to the French could be taken by interested agencies in Washington as a result of Roosevelt's negative and indefensible attitude. . . .

There is no need to question whether France benefited from de Gaulle's spectacular career; in the time of her moral and material bankruptcy, France found in de Gaulle the unique voice which summoned her to believe in the magnificent heritage of her past. Without de Gaulle to rally the French Empire and to serve as focal point and symbol of the Resistance, France might have fumbled throughout the war for means to unify her actions and failing, could have emerged hopelessly divided, seething with internal dissension. In spite of President Roosevelt's snide anecdotes, de Gaulle's place in French history, by the side of Joan of Arc, is undeniably secure.

De Gaulle's wisdom in choosing his methods of collaborating with the Allies is another matter. By scrupulously insisting that every French sovereign right be respected, de Gaulle forced England and America into recognition of the fact that even though defeated and deficient in power, France continued to exist. But let us suppose that de Gaulle had acted more pliantly regarding French interests: would the consequences have been such as to assist or weaken his aims? One may put in question de Gaulle's fundamental assumption that he must achieve the heights and never descend from them —the basic conviction of the idealist that forever stands in opposition to the pragmatist's concern for consequences. The opposition of idealism to pragmatism, ancient as the arguments of Plato and Aristotle, is vividly expressed in French history by the devotion of St. Joan and the cynical "Paris is worth a Mass" of Henry IV. Charles de Gaulle steered his course closer to Joan than to Henry, but he might have served France better by occasionally casting a tactful glance in the opposite direction when French issues were concerned. A more tolerant attitude in regard to Saint Pierre and Miquelon and the Levant states would have been worth cultivating even at the expense of neglecting French "rights." All the fury and bad blood developed over Syria and Lebanon did not alter the destiny of those states nor preserve French prerogatives within them. One can even propound the cynical suggestion that Vichy's strong-arm methods were more capable of preserving France's privileged position in Moslem areas than the liberalism (and military feebleness) of Free France. De Gaulle could easily and profitably have demonstrated better manners in regard to Churchill and Roosevelt. Anger at the Prime Minister and the President for trespassing on French soil was hardly worth cultivating at the expense of alienating the heads of two powerful states. And granted that de Gaulle stood within his rights over Strasbourg, the French stand on Stuttgart and the Italo-French boundary affairs[2] could hardly be justified from the point of view of enabling France to gain her ultimate objectives, which could be achieved better with assistance than with protests from London and Washington. With Allied good will and co-operation de Gaulle might have achieved a position which would have enabled him to protect French interests far more successfully than he could do when he butted headlong against the stone wall of Allied indignation.

The pattern of de Gaulle's relationship with the Allies, and especially with Roosevelt, is not without elements of tragedy, in its profoundest and grandest sense. Like Antigone, standing consistently, stubbornly, and proudly in defense of her convictions, de Gaulle aroused the world's admiration even as the implementation of his ideals foundered before the implacable opposition of great powers, corridor maneuvers, the importunity of human nature, and the reality of French political life. De Gaulle was at his best in 1940 when he called upon the French people to resist and at his most inexpert when faced five years later by the necessity of leading France through a complex of economic, political, and social reforms. Between 1940 and 1945, de Gaulle developed enormously from the unknown specialist in tank warfare to the statesman coping with international and domestic affairs; but in spite of a considerable and often unacknowledged diplomatic skill, he never acquired that magnanimity, that breadth of view, or that sense of humor which might have altered the tragic course of his career and rendered his achievement far greater than it was.

Whatever his defects, had there been no de Gaulle, there might have been no consistent pattern to American relations with France in World War II. Lacking the centralized force which de Gaulle brought to French dissidence, the historian would be compelled to describe a series of isolated incidents—the story of Pétain, of Admiral Robert, of Darlan, of Godefroy, of Giraud—with no unified pattern such as that provided by de Gaulle's personality and the program of Free France. De Gaulle's consistent adherence to his ideal imposed on the United States and the other Allies, in spite of themselves, the necessity of recognizing a France which, without his challenging leadership, might have been overlooked. To France, the loss of Charles de Gaulle would have been inestimable.

[2] De Gaulle pressured Eisenhower not to permit Strasbourg to be retaken by the Germans in January 1945, refused to allow French troops to hand control of Stuttgart to American forces assigned to its administration in April 1945, and used French troops to annex small areas of Italy in May 1945.—Ed.

The second Gaullism, de Gaulle's attempt in 1947–1953 to make the RPF the instrument of his return to power at the head of a coherent parliamentary majority, was a failure. FRANÇOIS GOGUEL (1909–   ), an influential French political scientist and author of such important books on French politics as *La Politique des partis sous la Troisième République*, attributes this failure to the tactics of the RPF's organizers and to that doctrinaire idealism and inability to compromise that had made de Gaulle, in Goguel's view, a great wartime leader.*

Transformation of the RPF into a Party

When General de Gaulle created the RPF in the spring of 1947, he did not intend to add one more political party to those among which the French voters were already divided. Quite the contrary, he wanted to create an organization capable of transcending the old divisions of opinion by rallying Frenchmen of all beliefs into a common attempt to accomplish certain objectives essential for the public welfare. In his mind, the word *rassemblement* meant something quite different from the word *party*. Four years later, during the electoral campaign of June 1951, every indication was that the RPF had nevertheless become a party like the others, and even a more disciplined party than most of the groups which, from the Right Center to the Left, formed electoral coalitions both against it and the Communist party.

General de Gaulle's scheme faced from the start a serious obstacle in the unfavorable reaction of the Socialists and the less unanimous and more qualified opposition of the Popular Republicans. In order to attract the citizens faithful to the traditional, Socialist Left or those sympathetic to the MRP's attempt to synthesize the Right and the Left of earlier days, the RPF had to overcome the handicap presented by the hostility of the political organizations to which these citizens had given their votes in 1945 and 1946. Moreover, Gaullism gave priority among its objectives to the struggle against the "separatism" of the Communists. Except for an infinitesimal number of individual exceptions, the RPF could not count on the support of

* From François Goguel, *France under the Fourth Republic* (Ithaca, N.Y.: Cornell University Press, 1952), pp. 47–57. Copyright 1952 by Cornell University Press. Used by permission of Cornell University Press. Footnote omitted.

those Frenchmen who had rallied either earlier or more recently to the new incarnation of the extreme Left tradition which the Communist party represents. These difficulties did not exist in the Center (RGR),[1] and on the Right (PRL,[2] Independents, and Peasants). In addition, these political groups were less disciplined than those of the Left and the extreme Left. They did not try to prevent their members from joining the RPF and therefore placed no obstacles in the way of the RPF's penetration of the sectors of the population whose sentiments, opinions, and interests they represented. It was obvious from the start that the RPF would have great difficulty in transcending the traditional hostility between Left and Right, but it was less difficult for it to combine with the various conservative groups from the PRL to the RGR. This meant strengthening French conservatism by bringing back into its fold the voters who had turned toward the MRP in 1945 and 1946, not because of their convictions, but because of their hostility to communism. On the whole, that is precisely what happened at the municipal elections of October 1947, at least in the cities. But it was difficult for the RPF to consolidate this conservative victory because it could not remain content with it.

General de Gaulle sincerely intended to appeal to every shade of opinion and was sincere in denying that he was interested only in its conservative elements. Although the bulk of the votes cast for lists endorsed by the RPF in October 1947 came from the old Right, some came from proletarian areas which had usually been oriented to the extreme Left. This was a promising omen which

[1] *Rassemblement des Gauches Républicaines.*—Ed.

[2] *Parti Républicain de la Liberté.*—Ed.

permitted the RPF to hope that, despite the opposition of the left-wing parties, it would succeed eventually in winning over at least some of their supporters. In order to accomplish this, it was obviously necessary to adopt a program satisfying the aspirations of the proletariat and, therefore, almost necessarily displeasing to those groups desirous of maintaining the classic capitalistic economy.

In January 1948, in the industrial and mining city of Saint-Etienne, which had just gone over to the RPF thanks to many workers' votes, General de Gaulle delivered a speech devoted to this program. He called for reforms in the organization of industry so that it would have the character of an association between capital and labor, in order to abolish both class antagonisms and the old dependence of the worker on the boss, in order to place them on an equal footing, and in order to substitute for capitalism and its wage system a sort of co-operative system of remuneration. In spite of its lack of precision and the uncertainty of the measures envisaged for bringing it about (the RPF has never said whether it intended to make the association of capital and labor compulsory or whether it intended simply to encourage it by, for example, tax advantages), the program was bound to upset French managerial groups, who were jealous of their authority in their plants. There is no doubt that in many areas in the October 1947 elections management had used its influence and its financial resources for the benefit of Gaullist candidates. By announcing a program designed to enable the RPF to win the support of the workers, de Gaulle ran the risk of alienating some of those people to whom he owed his electoral victory in October. Moderate and Radical political circles were no less disturbed, as they have always been closely linked with business.

This new program, however, did nothing to change the attitudes of the unions, the Socialist party, or the MRP. The principle of the association of capital and labor was unacceptable to the Socialists because it put on one level the more or less distant owners of an enterprise and the people whose daily work makes it prosper, instead of giving the latter a preponderant role. As for the MRP, its own proposal for reforming French industry closely resembled the association of capital and labor although it used different terminology. But its working-class wing, supported by the Christian unions, was already inclined to regard this proposal as too mild. And the party as a whole could not acknowledge the similarity between its program and the RPF's, because it was anxious to remain on good terms with the Socialists by forestalling any suspicions that it would accept a reactionary, corporative, program. It preferred to view the association of capital and labor simply as a fraud. It goes without saying that for the Communists a reform designed to mitigate or even to abolish the class struggle could only meet with implacable hostility. In addition, the RPF's tendency to want to settle all problems of labor relations on the level of the plant disturbed the CFTC, the FO, and the CGT.[3] Even more than the opposition of the parties, the unanimous hostility of the unions was to limit effectively the appeal to the workers of the RPF's position opposing the traditional structure of capitalism.

This aspect of the RPF's program was

[3] *Confédération Française des Travailleurs Chrétiens,* the Catholic trade union; *Force Ouvrière,* the Socialist trade union; and *Confédération Générale du Travail,* the Communist trade union.—Ed.

not, however, the main reason for the increasing difficulties which arose between 1948 and 1951 between the RPF and many of the Moderate and Radical politicians who had been willing in 1947 to participate in electoral coalitions with the RPF. The main reason is the uncompromising and blunt tactics that the RPF tried to impose on them in Parliament. Moderate members of Parliament have always been very jealous of their freedom of action. The RPF wanted the members of its intergroup to follow the tactics prescribed by the RPF's executive council, where they were hardly represented. This could not very well be to their liking. In addition, the RPF's tactics were to maintain an intransigent opposition, which was different from the policy of those Moderates and Radicals who, since January 1947, had decided to co-operate with tripartism in the hope of thereby progressively increasing their influence over public policy. But the RPF refused on principle to collaborate with the parties of the Third Force. According to the RPF, the "regime of parties" established by the constitution of 1946 was inherently condemned to impotence, and the National Assembly had been deprived of its legitimate authority by the results of the municipal elections of 1947. A new Assembly had to be elected by a majority electoral system, and it should undertake to revise the constitution by increasing the authority of the President. The RPF was resolved to maintain its uncompromising attitude as long as these conditions were not fulfilled. It hoped to be able to prevent the Third Force from governing, and to cause a crisis that would be impossible to resolve without taking the RPF's wishes into consideration. The authentic Gaullists continually took this attitude in Parliament. They modified it only rarely: they agreed to ratify the Atlantic Pact of 1949, to vote for measures in December of 1947 and March 1950 aimed at the Communist party and its activities, and to approve the new electoral system for the Council of the Republic in 1948. They could never muster, however, enough Moderates and Radicals to defeat the governments of the enlarged Third Force, even while the latter was being bitterly fought by the Communists.

The RPF's tactics implied that the political, economic, and international difficulties which would inevitably arise during the long period between the anticipated collapse of the Third Force and the RPF's advent to power, could be regarded as insignificant. It revealed a doctrinaire spirit quite different from the pragmatism of many Moderates, and especially of the Radicals, whose sense of the state is not compatible with a long period of systematic opposition. It assumed the absolute impotence of the governments of the Center, and that it would be impossible for the deputies whose aid was necessary to the Socialists and the Popular Republicans in forming a majority to make their views at least partially prevail. It clashed with the experience of the Third Republic, during which the Moderates had been able to play a significant role, not through intransigent opposition and refusal to accept the political system, but through conciliation and support of the existing institutions. Lastly, and this was undoubtedly not the least important consideration which led the Moderates and the Radicals to rebel against the RPF, General de Gaulle's personality and the memory of the way he had governed when he was in office disturbed many of the politicians. They feared that he was incapable of leading a parliamentary government during normal times because of the very qualities—his absolute refusal to agree at home or abroad to compromise over what he considered to be essential, and his absolute confidence in his own judgment—which had enabled him to play such an important role during the war.

The inability of the RPF to find the Moderate and Radical support in Parliament on which it had counted and without which its tactics were doomed to fail led it continually to toughen its attitude and its methods. The RPF's leaders saw that they could impose discipline only on the members of Parliament who had had to abandon their own party in order to rally to Gaullism. Experience revealed that the practice of double membership, on which the RPF had been based at its formation, was a double-edged weapon. The Gaullists of the Radical party, of the UDSR,[4] of the Peasant party, of the Independent group, and of the PRL, had not succeeded in orienting the activity of their groups in the direction desired by the RPF, and many of them paid greater heed to the position of their old parties than to that adopted by the intergroup on orders from the secretariat of the RPF. The RPF reached the point where it no longer really counted on the members of Parliament who were not entirely devoted to Gaullism. The role of the intergroups in the two assemblies continually decreased in importance in comparison with the exclusively RPF groups which had been created. One result of these developments was that it drove away from the RPF those people who had originally joined it with the intention of promoting greater understanding among the parties and who considered that its increased intransigence was becoming a

[4] *Union Démocratique et Socialiste de la Résistance.*—Ed.

divisive factor instead. All these changes did not take place at once, however, and it is useful to trace their principal stages.

An attempt was made several months after the municipal election of 1947, in February–March 1948, to bring about an understanding between the RPF and the Third Force for the purpose of creating a Broad union of national parties. The author of this attempt was René Pleven, the president of the UDSR, who had served with de Gaulle on the Committee of National Liberation and in the provisional government. Through press conferences, speeches, and numerous conversations, he tried to foster a movement in favor of conciliation. Robert Schuman, then Premier, was careful not to discourage him. Within the MRP and especially in the Socialist party, reservations were frequently expressed about the aims of Pleven's scheme. But it definitely failed because Pleven received no encouragement from the RPF. On the contrary, General de Gaulle continued to demand the immediate dissolution of the National Assembly, while the main advantage of the *rapprochement* desired by Pleven would have been to avoid the excitement and the loss of time of an electoral campaign and to guarantee the government a very large majority in Parliament and in the country. Pleven, seeing that his efforts would fail because of the RPF's refusal to participate, stopped his conciliatory efforts after a few weeks.

In April, 1948, Gabriel Cudenet, the president of the RGR, stated his opposition to a dissolution in which he saw only an "element of agitation." Although it did not commit all the members of the RGR, this attitude revealed the desire of the Radicals to stand apart from the RPF after having exploited it in the fall for electoral purposes. When,

in July 1948, the formation of the André Marie–Paul Reynaud cabinet clearly demonstrated the increase in influence of the Radicals and the Moderates, the RPF's policy of opposition raised still more doubts on the Right and in the Center of the National Assembly. It was at this time that Pierre Montel, a PRL deputy from the Rhône and vice-president of the Gaullist intergroup, resigned from the RPF.

The growing tendency of the RPF to renounce the idea of double membership in favor of becoming a party in the strict sense was emphasized in December by the formation, on the initiative of René Capitant, a member of the UDSR, of the purely RPF Group for Democratic and Social Action, which was joined by several members of the UDSR, Moderates, and former Popular Republicans. At the same time, after the renewal of the Council of the Republic, an RPF Group for Democratic and Republican Action was formed in the second chamber. The discipline of this group was soon going to contrast greatly with the lack of discipline of the intergroup, which was created at the same time and which was twice as large.

In January 1949, Jean Masson, a Radical deputy from Haute-Marne, resigned from the intergroup and declared that the RPF now deserved the criticism of monolithism that it directed at the parties. In June, the UDSR congress, over which René Pleven presided, dealt with the problem of Capitant's deviations by deciding to prohibit its members from remaining members of the RPF. A few weeks later, disputes arose over a local election in Seine-et-Marne. The Gaullist members of Parliament from the department had supported a different candidate than the one named by the RPF's central office, and they were reprimanded for it. Shortly after this incident, Paul Giacobbi, a Radical deputy and one of de Gaulle's former ministers, resigned from the RPF intergroup of which he was the president and said that "the RPF is killing the Rassemblement."

The RGR's break with Gaullism was then just about complete, but the Moderates' break with de Gaulle was not completed until the fall of 1949. At this time, the methodical and persevering organizational activities of the National Center of Independents were crowned by a successful congress. De Gaulle observed with ill humor this reconstitution of a conservative party which might cut into the votes and the membership of the RPF. A few days later he sarcastically remarked that he wondered on whom the self-styled Independents actually depended, an illusion to the rumors that business organizations were supporting financially this reorganization of the old Right.

Both when the Bidault cabinet was formed, and later when the Socialists withdrew from it, the RPF tried to reach an agreement with the MRP, undoubtedly in order to alleviate the effects of the growing tension in its relations with the RGR and the Moderates. The Popular Republicans reacted coldly to these advances, however, and nothing positive resulted from them.

The transformation which had taken place since the spring of 1948 in the RPF's relations with the parties whose activities it had wanted to harmonize and co-ordinate was illustrated most significantly in July 1950, when René Pleven, in the course of the debate which followed the formation of his cabinet, replied to René Capitant, who had reminded him of his conciliatory efforts in the spring of 1948, that in his eyes

"the RPF had become an obstacle to the union of the French."

In the fall, Jacques Soustelle, the secretary general of the RPF, speaking of the future elections, said that what was important for the RPF would be less the number of its deputies than their cohesion and their discipline. This was a formula that was obviously inspired by the RPF's disappointment in the members of Parliament who had flirted with it, and who had not followed its orders when they cast their votes in Parliament. This formula also explicitly betrayed the conversion of the old *rassemblement* into a party. One day in the course of the following winter General de Gaulle himself let the expression "our party" slip from his lips when he was talking about the RPF.

The Radical Socialist party drew the logical conclusion from the RPF's evolution by deciding, in the spring of 1951, to prohibit its members from also belonging to the RPF. It was already so alienated from the RPF that this decision did not provoke the resignation of more than two or three members of Parliament whom everyone had for long known were more Gaullist than Radical.

The results of the evolution since 1947 in the structure, methods, and in the very nature of the RPF could have been, however, offset at the time of the election of 1951. The mechanism of the alliance designed to permit the coalition of the majority parties without infringing upon their independence or even mitigating the contradictions of their respective programs could just as well have been used to create a coalition of the RPF, the Moderates, and the RGR. In many cases the latter two groups, preoccupied as they were with defeating not only communism but socialism, would have willingly agreed to ally their lists with those of the Gaullists. Frequently, even the MRP would have joined these alliances, but, despite the entreaties of its potential partners and contrary to the advice of many of its local representatives, the RPF decided to agree only in exceptional cases to make alliances and to go into the electoral battle alone almost everywhere.

This decision gave one advantage to the RPF in that it was not again identified with the Right, an advantage of which the RPF had become aware during the developments from 1948 to 1951. It also enabled the RPF to present itself as a third solution for those people who opposed communism and who wanted something new because of the ineffectiveness of the governments which had succeeded one another since 1946. It permitted it to deny that it participated, as did the parties that it opposed, in jockeying for purely electoral considerations. Finally, it assured the RPF's secretariat that its candidates were completely loyal and would maintain party discipline. This desire for isolation, which was broken, for local reasons, in only twelve districts out of a hundred, ended by giving the RPF the appearance of a closed, monolitic, and rigorously disciplined party, instead of the rallying point for various parties which it was supposed to be when it was created. For this very reason, the Moderates and Radicals who had never supported the Third Force governments were compelled to join with the Third Force parties, at least for electoral purposes, in order to form the alliances on which the new electoral law placed a premium. The pressure that was, perhaps involuntarily, exerted by the RPF because of its electoral isolation contributed to a great extent to bringing together in the elections not only the Socialists, the Popular Republicans, and their allies of the enlarged Third Force majority, but also all those members of the opposition who had refused to accept the rigorous discipline of the RPF and to subordinate everything to General de Gaulle's accession to power.

In outward appearance, the French political situation was thus clarified by the formation of three major groups, two of which, the RPF and the Communist party, opposed a coalition of all the other parties loyal to parliamentary democracy. Actually, the diversity of the programs of the various elements of the third group was going to create after the elections a more confusing and less stable situation than had ever existed between 1946 and 1951.

Writing in 1950 of de Gaulle's leadership of the RPF, H. STUART HUGHES (1916–   ), who is professor of history at Harvard University and author of works on European intellectual history such as *Consciousness and Society: The Reorientation of European Social Thought, 1890–1930,* concludes that de Gaulle's political aims placed him in the historical tradition of "Bonaparte-Boulanger-Pétain," but that the new movement, far from being anachronistic, should be regarded as a mild, French form of fascism.*

A French Form of Fascism

In the small hours of the morning of New Year's Day 1946, General de Gaulle, president-premier of France and undisputed first citizen of his country, abruptly offered his resignation to the First Constituent Assembly. In words that carried a tone of both reproof and menace, he warned the astonished deputies that they had embarked on a wrong course:

"We have begun to reconstruct the Republic. You will continue to do so. However you do it, I think I can tell you in all conscience . . . that if you do it without taking into account the lessons of our political history of the past fifty years and, in particular, of what happened in 1940, if you do not take into account the absolute necessity for

governmental authority, dignity, and responsibility, you will reach a situation such that sooner or later, I predict, you will bitterly regret having taken the road which you will have taken. . . .

"Yes, there are two conceptions. They are not reconcilable. . . .

"Do we want a government which governs or do we want an omnipotent Assembly selecting a government to accomplish its will? This second solution means a regime which we ourselves have sometimes tried, and others also have done so.

"Personally, I am convinced that it does not in any sense answer to the necessities of the country in which we live, nor to those of our era, in which problems are so numerous, so complex,

* Reprinted from H. Stuart Hughes, "Gaullism: Retrospect and Prospect," in *Modern France: Problems of the Third and Fourth Republics* edited by Edward Meade Earle, by permission of Princeton University Press. Copyright 1951 by Princeton University Press. Footnotes omitted.

so rapid, so brutal, that it appears impossible to solve them within any such constitutional framework. . . .

"The formula which is forced upon us . . . is a government which has and which bears alone—I say: alone—the entire responsibility for the executive power."

Although de Gaulle's actual resignation did not come until three weeks later, his declarations on that tense New Year's Day had established a position from which there was no turning back and which virtually obliged him to withdraw from the government. To many of his followers and well-wishers his resignation came as a painful shock. Five months later, they sustained another shock when the General signalized his return to active participation in national affairs by his blunt constitutional pronouncement at Bayeux. And before another year had gone by, de Gaulle was to shake them again with his assumption of an active political role at the head of his Rassemblement du Peuple Français. To many Frenchmen, these sudden irruptions on the political scene seemed nothing but the intemperate products of frustrated personal ambition. Some saw in them the fulfillment of long-deferred hopes—others the confirmation of inherited fears. Few recognized their inner logic and historical consistency.

De Gaulle's declarations on the night of December 31, 1945, pointed both forward and back. They recalled his experiences of resistance and exile in London and Algiers. They charted his future political course. Three things in particular emerge: the suggestion of a program that linked up with a long tradition and could strike a sympathetic chord among numerous and influential segments of the French population; the exploitation of a very special personal situation and a carefully cultivated *mystique;* a consistency with the speaker's past and his actions to come.

I

It was no hard task for de Gaulle's critics to connect his forthright political declarations with the tradition summarized in the names Bonaparte-Boulanger-Pétain. Even certain of the General's friends did not deny the association. The young and ardent Jean de Borcey, related to de Gaulle both "by blood and by a faithful and fraternal affection," wrote of the liberation of France as a *"Brumaire"*—an opportunity that the General had most regrettably let slip but that fortunately had presented itself again. Political observers soon noted that it was the former Pétainists who flocked in the greatest numbers in response to the new rallying-cry. The statistics of the local elections of October 1947 and March 1949 proved that there was no other party for which any considerable number of Pétainists could be voting, nor any other large constituency (except the floaters of the MRP)[1] which was free to rally to de Gaulle. Leftists critics have exulted with impunity at the proliferation of aristocratic and wealthy names in the Gaullist ranks. As conservative a journal as *Le Monde* has found a parallel between the urban enthusiasm for Boulanger and de Gaulle's victories in the large cities in 1947. American scholars have endorsed the Bonapartist precedent. All this seems proved beyond contradiction. The chord had been touched that vibrates in response to appeals to the family, religion, the army, the constituted orders of society, the state, and national unity. Those who had never accepted the Republic had again found their man. The

[1] *Mouvement Républicain Populaire,* the French Christian Democratic Party.—Ed.

classes, the interests, the social leaders that at moments of crisis have sought a solution in military authoritarianism, by the summer of 1947 had rallied to de Gaulle.

At the same time, those who formed the rank and file of the Free French following in the Resistance years—the Socialists and the Communists, and, to a lesser extent, the MRP—had become the General's bitterest opponents. Some observers have seen a malign illogicality in this reversal of roles, and have accused de Gaulle of opportunism, and the French Left and moderate Left of blindness during the war years. I shall take up later the charge of inconsistency. The question of the attitude of French democrats—and more particularly of the Socialists—toward de Gaulle in London and Algiers is more complex and pressing.

If one should ask a French Socialist today whether he regretted the support he gave de Gaulle in the war years, he would no doubt answer in the negative. He would recall that the General offered the only rallying-point, the only symbol of resistance, up to the very moment of Liberation. He would reconstruct the circumstances of the time—and especially the need for national unity in the face of Vichy and near-Vichy intrigue and the doubtful attitude of the United States. Above all, he would insist that it was not to the General as an individual that he had given his support, but to the Free French movement in its largest and most democratic sense. About de Gaulle himself he had always has his reservations, and he had tried to the extent of his power to counteract the influence of the General's personal entourage and to steer the movement as a whole into more democratic channels.

It is in this sense that a fair-minded critic will judge the activities of such

men as Félix Gouin and André Philip in London and Algiers. Their efforts were directed toward building up the Consultative Assembly as a counter-weight to de Gaulle the leader. Whether the Assembly proved in practice to be anything more than a sham is another question. Again, more of that later. In any case, as an attempt at parliamentary democracy in a situation in which a functioning parliamentary system was obviously out of the question, the Consultative Assembly became "an institution unique among the western governments-in-exile."

Yet one cannot deny that the spectacle of de Gaulle-Cincinnatus abruptly transforming himself into de Gaulle-Bonaparte rather surpassed the reasoned anticipations of French parliamentary democrats. Since 1947, we have acquired a new focus on the conflicts of the Resistance period.

II

In this new focus, the stories, the rumors, that circulated in anti-Gaullist circles during the war years have taken on increased verisimilitude and a heightened actuality. The Duke Street torture chamber in London; the unexplained circumstances of the deaths of the Resistance leaders Moulin (Monsieur X) and Médéric; the machinations of the Gaullist intelligence service, the BCRA; the Cagoulard past of several of the General's closest associates and his own authoritarian leanings—to all these we are likely to give more credence than we did six or seven years ago.[2] We may read with more approbation now Henri de Kerillis' account of his unsuccessful efforts to induce de Gaulle to undertake the rescue from captivity of such prominent pre-1940 leaders as Reynaud,

[2] Unproven charges of strong-arm intimidation by de Gaulle's supporters.—Ed.

Gamelin, Mandel, Daladier, and Blum, and can comprehend the reasons for the General's coolness to the proposal. We understand more clearly now the disappointment of the 100 per cent Gaullists—freely admitted by Colonel Passy himself—at Bidault's selection as chairman of the National Council of Resistance in Paris instead of a Gaullist nominee, and, after the liberation of Paris, the protracted and difficult negotiations between Bidault and the General over the reconstruction of the Provisional Government. And we see why it was a matter of vital necessity to the Algiers government that Leclerc's armored division should be on hand for the liberation of the capital—not only for reasons of national prestige but to influence the crucial political decisions that would be made there.

In this perspective, also, the experience of the Algiers Consultative Assembly appears less promising than it did at the time. We recall the doubts as to whether the "mandate" of the Resistance deputies was much more than a patriotic fiction, and the frequent complaint that these deputies were men of second rank, who could be spared for sterile political activity while the real Resistance leaders remained in France— even the former, critics added, had been screened for Gaullist orthodoxy before being given facilities for reaching Algiers. Tales such as these have remained on the level of gossip and polemic and still lack impartial confirmation. But as to the comedy—or scandal, if one prefers— of the election of certain overseas deputies, there is no reason for doubt; de Gaulle's personal intervention in the selection of a delegate from the French community of New York soon became common knowledge. By one means or another, the Gaullist inner circle had assured itself of a safe majority.

When we think back now on the sessions of that Assembly, we realize more clearly than before that though the new institution might provide a parliamentary façade, behind it the General's personal authority remained nearly intact. His stalwarts "of the first hour"—most of whom lacked either Resistance or party standing—still held roughly half the ministries. His conduct of war and diplomacy, and more particularly his politically tinged orders to the Resistance forces in France, remained outside the Assembly's sphere of action. Meantime the Consultative occupied itself with somewhat academic projects for the reestablishment of "republican legality" on the liberation of the home country. De Gaulle's appearances before that body carried a dramatic, almost a plebiscitary tone—for all his efforts to temper his remarks to the sensibilities of old parliamentarians. And—inevitable accompaniment to these scenes—to quote Gordon Wright's elegant description, de Gaulle's "closest confidant, Gaston Palewski, . . . would be seen a few feet away, always lounging against the same pillar, his thoughts masked by a smile that seemed to combine Machiavelli and Mona Lisa." Palewski was a conservative and a believer in strong government; his constant attendance on de Gaulle suggested that such were the views of the inner circle and of the chief himself. The parliamentarians, the Socialists and the radical democrats, essentially remained outside.

The foregoing presents perhaps too hostile a picture. In answer, de Gaulle's defenders have always maintained that whatever imperiousness there was in his wartime conduct arose from the unavoidable necessities of his country's situation: a strong center of authority, a curbing of dissidence and half-loyalty, was required to stop the Communist drive for the *noyautage*[3] of the whole Resistance. They add that it was de Gaulle himself who, against the wishes of many of the Resistance leaders, decided for the revival of the pre-war political parties within the French underground. The two viewpoints are not entirely incompatible, and there is validity in both of them. One thing, however, is certain. Even de Gaulle's most circumspect apologists have not denied that the General and his friends sedulously exploited the circumstances of the Resistance experience to build up the *mystique* that has remained de Gaulle's most persistent attribute.

This *mystique* is the lasting legacy of the Resistance period. The Gaullist inner circle achieved a notable success in seizing a sentiment that was merely vague and diffused and concentrating it on the person of their leader. Scenes of frenzied devotion and rhythmic crowd chanting of *"Vive de Gaulle!"* became regular occurrences during and immediately following the Liberation. And already—I cite a personal experience from September of 1945—indignant old-line Republicans were protesting that the crowd should be shouting *"Vive la France!"* instead. By 1945—and indeed all through the war period—the fearful and the clairvoyant had sensed the menace of authoritarian government.

III

Thus we arrive at de Gaulle's logical consistency. There is a continuing thread that connects the boy who "before the age of twelve, . . . had reached the conclusion that destiny had chosen him to guide the nation in a future hour of crisis," with the soldier who labored to solve the technical problems of his country's defense, the exiled leader in London

and Algiers striving to rebuild the concept of national independence and dignity around his own person, the scornful, principled opponent of the two draft constitutions of 1946, and finally, the political chief who has suffused with his spirit an equivocal mass movement. In these successive stages, one period stands out as different from the rest—the experience as a semiconstitutional chief of state from the election of the First Constituent Assembly in October 1945 to his resignation three months later. It was a position in which he was never entirely happy, if we may believe one of his apologists, who complains that this Assembly, and in particular its disciplined parties, cut the General off from the country as the Consultative had never done. In retrospect, the experiment in parliamentary constitutionalism appears as a mere episode. By retiring from power and simultaneously stating his long-held constitutional convictions, de Gaulle resumed his familiar role.

These convictions, as stated in the now classic speeches of Bayeux, Épinal, and Lille, have scarcely altered in the three succeeding years. A recent article by Gaston Palewski—who can be presumed to be speaking for his master—cites them as gospel. Their main features are familiar: a strong presidency; a second chamber virtually coequal with the Assembly, and based partly on a system of corporate representation; a strict separation of legislative and executive functions; a federal constitution for the Empire, assuring in practice the preponderance of the French state. A curious feature of this program is its rejection of popular election for the president—presumably in order to take some of the sting from the Bonapartist parallel. The president is rather to be chosen by a large electoral college or series of colleges. At the same time, the plebiscitary

---

[3] Swamping, i.e. Communist takeover.—Ed.

feature appears in another form: in cases of grave conflict between the executive and the legislative the president may call for a national referendum. Or, alternatively, he may dissolve the Assembly and thus bring on new elections. This threat of dissolution is the really powerful weapon that de Gaulle's constitutional project places in the hands of the president.

The resulting structure, Palewski explains, would be neither a parliamentary constitution on the British model nor a full-fledged presidential system, like the American. It would combine features of both. Its most debatable aspect, he implies, is the president's dual role as director of the executive, "that is, one of the [three separate] powers," and as "arbiter between these powers." In explaining this seeming paradox, Palewski gets to the very center of the Gaullist concept: ". . . [the president's] supervision is to be felt chiefly in the areas which are traditionally the sphere of the chief of state;—those which are closely connected with his role as guardian of the integrity of the national territory and of respect for treaties: foreign policy, national defense, the French Union. . . ."

With this, we are back to de Gaulle's earliest and most persistent interests: the strength and integrity of the French state facing an external menace. In the event of war, the executive authority, the military forces, the resources of the Empire, must all be closely knit together. In case of necessity, France overseas must be suitably organized to become again the temporary base of national resistance; under such circumstances of crisis, no divisive nationalist agitation in the colonies may be tolerated. And the crisis is already upon us: qualified witnesses report that the Liberation was hardly accomplished before de Gaulle became convinced that a third world war was inevitable—and imminent. He resolved that never again shall France find herself in the position of administrative and military paralysis into which she had drifted under the constitution of 1875.

IV

There is a second central line of thought in Palewski's exegesis—and one that serves as an introduction to the internal—as opposed to the foreign and military—aspects of de Gaulle's program and appeal. It is the familiar "wave of the future" argument, clothed in technological language: the technical necessities of our time demand that power rest in "firm and sure hands." This argument recalls the General's parting blast at the First Constituent Assembly. It also recalls the Resistance experience and one of the nearly forgotten smaller Resistance movements. In the years 1942 to 1943, the OCM (Organisation Civile et Militaire), a group dominated by intellectuals and higher civil servants and notably loyal to de Gaulle, had clandestinely circulated plans for the constitutional reconstruction of France. In a spirit which critics attacked as "technocratic," the OCM had proposed a presidential system on the American model, with a cabinet responsible to the president alone. Such a concentration of power went beyond what de Gaulle himself currently advocates. Perhaps it was truer to the spirit and ultimate implications of the General's program than his own more modest proposal.

A more dispassionate and closely reasoned version of the technological argument appears in a semi-academic article published a few weeks after the launching of the RPF. Its author, Paul-Émile Viard, deputy from Algiers and former dean of the Algiers Law Faculty, professes to speak as an independent, saddened by the advent of political Gaullism but convinced that it answers to the needs of his time. De Gaulle's recent gesture, he argues, "corresponds in an imperious fashion to the evolution of present-day institutions." Parliamentarism no longer functions; symbolic of its hollowness is the new system whereby the whip of each parliamentary group in the Assembly votes his party *en bloc*. The great organized pressure groups actually run the state, which lacks a center of administrative unity. Under these circumstances, Viard concludes, we must either return to the classic parliamentarism of the nineteenth century— liberal in politics and economics—

"Or else we shall continue to indulge in the play of parties, of established corporate bodies, of powerful trade-unions, of growing provisions for special status, of the *mystique* of numbers, and of quasi-socialist *dirigisme*. In this case, the political system will call for an executive to recreate the principle of unity.

"Within this second hypothesis—alas, the more probable!—another dilemma arises: either the reform will be carried out in an all-inclusive and rapid fashion by de Gaulle—with or without the RPF —and in this case it will be carried out under conditions of order, liberty, and harmonious political organization, or his attempt will fail and . . . the reform will be carried out just the same, sooner or later, by someone else, after crises and convulsions which the country could very well do without."

V

The balancing, the reconciliation of great pressure groups by a strong executive: such is the essence of the Gaullist formula. Through the euphemisms of the General's official propaganda, this reality emerges. Is this Fascism? How-ever much we may want to avoid an emotional and much-abused word, we must meet the question honestly. De Gaulle's critics are quite sure that he and his movement are Fascist; his supporters either deny it or evade the issue. This polemic gets us nowhere. In a case such as this, where the significant facts are established and well known, the argument may be largely verbal—a sterile dispute over an ugly label.

If we mean by Fascism the more sinister doctrines and practices that characterized the Mussolini and, in particular, the Hitler régimes—racism, predatory war, mass brutality, and a thoroughgoing police supervision of private life—then the epithet is undeserved, or at the least premature. These may be the eventual implications of the Gaullist program. Once in power, the General might feel obliged to resort to them. For the present, there is no compelling reason for doubting his word when he rejects them. It is even too early to say whether de Gaulle would actually scrap his own constitutional proposals and the traditional liberties of his people and would govern France as a dictator. We should not rule out the possibility that he means what he says, that he sincerely believes his semipresidential system would equip his country with a sufficient measure of executive authority.

Yet even with this narrower—and perhaps excessively charitable—definition of Gaullism, the term Fascist may apply. If we give to the word what we might call a Latin connotation (one deriving from the experience of Italy and Spain rather than of Germany), then Fascism is practically the equivalent of the corporate state. And what has the corporate state proved to be in practice if not the balancing and integration in a nationalist sense of great pressure groups by a strong executive? We should add, of course, that in such an integration, it is the capitalist as opposed to the working class groups that win out. This is not the corporatism of Catholic theorists—although that too appears in de Gaulle's formal program in his advocacy of the "association" of workers in the ownership of factories. But traditional corporatism has by now become little more than a rather touching memory of blasted hopes. Rather than a true reconciliation of conflicting economic and social pressures, it has demonstrated itself in practice to be an admirable device for clothing the realities of class domination in the trappings of national unity.

In this sense, we may call Gaullism either Fascist or corporative as we prefer. It may be objected that this is an oversimplification—that Gaullism is a curious and personal amalgam peculiar to the General himself and to his country. But cannot the same be said of Fascism everywhere? While Fascism is a universal and international phenomenon of our century, it has never appeared twice in the same form. Peculiarities of time, national tradition, and leading personalities have marked each of its manifestations. Even in the same country, slight differences of circumstance may effect crucial changes in a Fascist movement's prospects of success. We have seen how Gaullism has been marked from the start by its leader's Resistance record and his long and consistent advocacy of a strong and coherent national policy. Thus Gaullism suggests the very opposite of that antipatriotism and collusion with the enemy which unavoidably limited the appeal of Pétainism.

Moreover, the characteristic stigmata

of Fascist movements are not lacking in Gaullist tactics and the Gaullist appeal. We find the familiar defense of law and order and the old ruling classes—a position which, as J. E. Sawyer has pointed out, the General assumed as early as the moment of liberation in opposition to the revolutionary aspirations of the Resistance Left. From here, it was only a logical step for de Gaulle to stand forth as the protector of all but the most notorious of former collaborationists. Coupled with this—in apparent contrast but conforming to a more subtle logic— we find the successful appeal to the salaried petty bourgeoisie, embittered by a postwar inflation in which prices have outrun incomes. Along with these class appeals, comes the familiar attack on "money"—a transparent sign of the Fascist type of manipulation when used by a party whose large capitalist source of funds is common knowledge. We find the customary shock-troop cadres, the emotionally charged public meetings, the sudden and dramatic practice mobilizations. And—perhaps the most pervasive symptom—we recognize the lack of clear doctrine, the simple-minded or calculated political obfuscation. Anyone who needs to be convinced of Gaullism's intellectual feebleness has only to read the little book in which James Burnham records his interview with André Malraux. The latter, the intellectual *vedette* of the movement, has nothing more lucid to offer than a faith not "in programs, but only in objectives" and the "myth" of "a new human type: the liberal hero." Again we bow to the shade of Georges Sorel....

RAYMOND ARON (1905–   ), professor of sociology at the University of Paris and one of France's leading commentators on political and economic affairs, was editor of the Gaullist monthly *Free France* during the war and a member of the National Council of the RPF. Although he later came to feel that Gaullism had lost some of its doctrinal strength, in 1948 in *The Great Schism,* he argued that de Gaulle had none of the characteristics of a fascist leader. On the contrary, he claimed, de Gaulle had the vision to see how freedom could be safeguarded in the age of mass democracy and state economic planning.*

► |||||| *A Novelty Full of Promise*

Shall we say that the double, concerted opposition of the Rally and of the Communists is similar to that of communism and fascism against democracy? I do not know what will become of the RPF if it reaches power. For the moment, the comparison with fascism misses fundamental differences. It is true that the RPF belongs to the species of Bonapartist movements which, from Napoleon I to Boulanger, passing by Napoleon III, have arisen in France in the course of the preceding centuries when the country was weary of parliamentary chaos and monarchical restoration was debarred. Again this time, the regrouping is formed around a man whose political itinerary has passed from

Left to Right, who restored the Republic before gathering troops for the most part from the Right.

But in relation to the Bonapartism of the preceding century, the RPF is distinguished first by the character of its leader. General de Gaulle has once been in power. If he committed errors, if his economic administration was neither better nor worse than that of his successors, he showed as much care for legality as for authority. He has no taste at all for parliamentarians and their subtleties, or for power without limits and without rules. The regime he dreams of would be closer to presidential democracy than to despotism.

The Rally itself has nothing in com-

---

* From Raymond Aron, *Le Grand schisme* (Paris: Editions Gallimard, 1948), pp. 225–226, 259–269. Translated by editor.

mon with a totalitarian party. It has neither the structure, organization, doctrine, nor propaganda that would permit it to win over and fanaticize millions of men. It permits double allegiance. In the municipal elections, Radicals and members of the PRL[1] joined together on the lists of RPF candidates, without their party membership being erased by their common candidature. One ought to criticize the organizational weakness of the Rally rather than its rigidity.

It incontestably receives, in large part, the votes of the Right. But its staff, sprung from the Resistance, comes partly from the Left. Besides, what do the words Left and Right mean henceforth, since the extreme Left intends to establish a totalitarian regime and despises freedom? Except by reference to the social situation and to the former orientation of its troops, one could not say that the RPF is more or less to the Right than the Third Force.[2]

What is true is that the RPF is a reaction to a crisis and a threat which, during the period between the two wars, the fascists vainly claimed to be overcoming: the crisis is that of parliamentary democracy in the age of the masses and of the economy under state direction, the threat that of communist totalitarianism. The fascists have found no other solution than that of anti-communist totalitarianism. To the myth of proletarian liberation they opposed that of national grandeur. As a result of imperial dreams, they flung the world into a deluge of blood and ruined the Europe they were claiming to unite. Even if they wanted to do so, the Gaullists would be quite incapable of recon-

stituting fascism because the peoples are no longer impressed by nationalist exaltation. . . .

The RPF, by its very existence, is in the process of modifying the structure of the political parties. Absorbing the old formations, the isolated groups, into a vast rally, capable of becoming a governmental majority, it is simplifying the political scene and ending anachronistic quarrels. It has brought the parties in power, by the pressure it exerts on them, to forget for a while that some go to Mass and that others don't. Radicals and moderates, moderates and MRP (I am speaking of the troops, not of the general staffs) find themselves on the same candidate list, or vote for the same men. It is said that the troops of the RPF are heterogeneous, and this criticism is well-founded, since its troops extend from extreme Right to moderate socialists, but what meaning do these nuances still have? What are the true differences between a PRL and a Radical, between an MRP and a Radical? Some are not more anti-communist than others, and all declare they are republicans, and even supporters of the parliamentary republic. One can say that some are more liberal than others in economic matters, some hostile to and some favorable to nationalization, but no party is homogeneous in this matter. The MRP, and probably the Socialist party itself, has its supporters of state control and its liberals. No one wants to rush into new nationalization; everyone wants to reform the operation of those industries that have been nationalized since the Liberation. Is it said that a group of the RPF inclines toward fascist methods and that another remains faithful to the republic? Let us admit it. These theoretical divisions matter much less than the contradictions in the situa-

[1] *Parti Républicain de la Liberté,* a conservative group.—Ed.

[2] Coalition of the Socialists, MRP, and Radicals.—Ed.

tion itself. Will parliament succeed in adapting itself to the needs of our society, to the difficulties of the struggle against communist sabotage? On the reply to that question depends the survival of democratic institutions much more than on the ideologies of such and such a Gaullist.

Indeed, what is called the "heterogeneity" of its troops is the fact that different spiritual families find themselves together within the RPF; Christian Democrats, conservative Catholics, and Radicals have all voted for the Rally. So, what is deplored and denounced as a sort of confusion, seems to me on the contrary to be a novelty full of promise. To forbid different interest groups to coalesce and different philosophies of existence to express themselves, that is fascism. To found the State on coalitions of interest groups and on rival philosophies, that is to bring about its ruin. The Democratic and Republican parties in the United States, the Labour and Conservative parties in Great Britain, group together many political leanings. If each of these were to be organized into a separate political party, the Anglo-Saxon democracies would become pluralist in the French manner. It is doubtful if they would gain anything by doing so.

Thus, events perhaps favor the realization of the three conditions indispensable to the survival of Western democracies in our century: the elimination of the Communist party, the restoration of the power of the State over intermediary bodies, and the creation of a coherent majority.

Circumstances will bring about someday, in three weeks, in three months, or in three years, the breakdown of the present system. The RPF and General de Gaulle appear as the probable beneficiaries of this breakdown. Are they simply an expedient for a few months or for several years for getting out of the crisis? Or will they be able to restore the State to the point of making themselves of no further use?

One of the most reliable accounts of the events leading to de Gaulle's investiture as premier in June 1958 is given in the following excerpt from *De Gaulle's Republic* by British political scientists PHILIP M. WILLIAMS (1920–   ), author of *Crisis and Compromise: Politics in the Fourth Republic,* and MARTIN HARRISON (1930–   ). By reconstructing in detail the events of May 13–June 1, 1958, in Algeria, Corsica, and France, the authors indicate the importance in de Gaulle's return to power of the manipulation of the Algiers revolt by a group of Gaullist conspirators and of de Gaulle's extremely skillful handling of the politicians in Paris. Their unstated conclusion thus seems to be that de Gaulle's strategy during these crucial two weeks is the supreme proof of his political realism.*

Cincinnatus Returns

[The defeat of the government of Félix Gaillard on April 15, 1958, in censure of its Algerian policy, opened a month-long political crisis in France, during which no political leader was able to win investiture as Premier in the National Assembly. Finally, on May 8, Pierre Pflimlin, who had persuaded the MRP not to support the candidature of Georges Bidault, one of its members who favored all-out war in Algeria, was asked to form a government.] So the choice fell on M. Pierre Pflimlin of MRP, a financial specialist with a reputation for liberal opinions on Algeria. His bid for the premiership, which was thought unlikely to succeed, was to be made on the thirteenth of May.

This cautious and responsible politician hardly seemed the man to provoke revolutionary opposition. But he had just stopped Bidault, and Algiers suspected he meant to negotiate with the FLN.[1] Four distinct groups there were determined to prevent him. They had little in common, and it was somewhat to their own surprise that they soon found themselves committed, as the standard-bearer of their resistance, to General de Gaulle.

The first group was the handful of wealthy *colons.*[2] Well connected in

[1] *Front de Libération Nationale*—National Liberation Front, the organization leading the Algerian rebellion against France.—Ed.

[2] European settlers.—Ed.

* From Philip M. Williams and Martin Harrison, *De Gaulle's Republic* (London: Longmans, Green & Co., Limited, 1961), pp. 45–47, 51–60, 64–65, 67–74. Footnotes omitted.

Parliament, expert lobbyists, plentifully supplied with funds by a levy on businesses and farms, they were experienced, resourceful, and determined in defence of their privileges. They had no love at all for de Gaulle; in the war they had preferred Pétain, or failing him Giraud. Until Gaillard's fall their spokesman, Alain de Sérigny, had been working for a "Government of Public Safety" under the "quartet." Not until 11 May did he come out for the General.

Next came the European poor. They were terrified of being abandoned by France. The rich could move home (and many had, since the war began). But their home was in Algeria, and often had been there for generations; they were fighting for its security. Among them were many different groups (usually led, of course, by men of the middle-class). The most active and ruthless were fascist in type. The largest, the UFNA, claimed 17,000 members. Its leader, Robert Martel, had been briefly interned by Lacoste;[3] he was in touch with Paris counter-revolutionaries. Also important were the Poujadists,[4] led by Dr. Bernard Lefèvre. Both organisations were active on 6 February 1956; from both came recruits for counter-terrorists like Kovacs. Likewise prominent in previous demonstrations had been the students' union (AGEA) led by Pierre Lagaillarde (whose predecessor had been called up by Lacoste for rioting against the loi-cadre),[5] and the secondary school-boys' union, AGELCA. The ex-servicemen, whose leaders were not as determined as the others to overthrow democracy in France, were less noisy but more

substantial. They alone might genuinely be attracted to de Gaulle's banner.

The third group was tiny: the knot of Gaullist conspirators. Handful though they were, they were not without assets. Many army officers had served with the Free French forces, and naturally preferred the Gaullists to their fascist rivals. Moreover, in France itself very many Gaullists had been in the state machine —administration, police, armed services —ever since liberation. Old Resistance and RPF contacts were readily renewed, and enabled the Gaullists to enjoy complicity and support at home, and especially in the government's own services, which the others could not match. Furthermore, the General himself still enjoyed immense prestige among Moslems. Thus once an explosion occurred, the Gaullists were well placed to take advantage of it. But they had few reliable followers in Algeria, and no certainty whatever that de Gaulle would give them his blessing.

The fourth force was decisive: the army. It contained several factions; some had Gaullist sympathies, others were in touch with the ultras. Few had any love for the rich colons, whose past neglect and exploitation of the Moslems they blamed for the war; Massu[6] had bitterly criticized Soustelle[7] for defeating the first loi-cadre, saying "These blind irresponsible fools will lose us Algeria." But deeper still was their mistrust of the politicians, whom they blamed for all the defeats and humiliations from 1940 to Suez; who allowed the despised Parisian intellectuals and journalists to traduce and vilify the army; who permitted Tunisia to aid the rebels, then let the Anglo-Saxons interfere with her just

[3] Minister for Algeria, 1956–1958.—Ed.

[4] Followers of Pierre Poujade, a conservative group favoring French Algeria.—Ed.

[5] A bill proposed in 1957 giving Moslem Algerians control of certain provinces and placing them on the same voting rolls as Europeans.—Ed.

[6] Paratroop general, military commander in the Algiers region.—Ed.

[7] Gaullist; one of the principal supporters of French Algiera.—Ed.

chastisement. The soldiers found political weakness in Paris a crippling handicap in their own military task. How could they convince the Moslems that France really meant to remain, when ministries and policies changed—for incomprehensible but doubtless sordid reasons—every six months? Sooner or later some politician, accidentally tossed up by a stray parliamentary wave, would propose to abandon the struggle, capitulate to the FLN, and force the army again to betray men who had trusted and worked for them. But the army would not stand being humiliated again. Algeria should not go the way of Tunisia and Morocco. And if the regime could not save it, then in Bidault's words, "Better mourn the Fourth Republic than *Algérie française*". . . .

The civilian extremists in Algiers would willingly have overthrown the Republic on or after 6 February 1956. The army opposed them; Massu, for instance, stopped their demonstration against the *loi-cadre* in September 1957. The thirteenth of May was made possible by the changed attitude of the military chiefs, and precipitated at that particular moment by the conduct of Lacoste.

The army's outlook changed essentially because of resentment at internationalization, fear of capitulation, and a growing conviction that the Fourth Republic was so incapable of consistency or determination that under it French Algeria was ultimately doomed. The man who exploited the soldiers' mood was Léon Delbecque. A self-made busiman, secretary of the RPF in Nord, he had served in Algeria as a reserve officer in 1956. When the Gaullist Chaban-Delmas became Minister of Defence under Gaillard at the end of 1957, Soustelle suggested that he should appoint Delbecque to his staff. Back in Algiers, Del-becque set himself to turn the explosion which he foresaw to the advantage of the General. Without revealing this aim, he preached the impotence of the regime to army officers, promoted contacts between them and the civilian malcontents, and after Gaillard's fall organized a Committee of Vigilance—to which twenty-two parties, student and ex-service groups adhered—to channel the popular discontent in the direction he desired. Its first demonstration—or rehearsal—was on 26 April. Its real blow was to be struck in the late summer.

Chaban-Delmas was aware of some of these activities (later he claimed credit for them all). Lacoste knew something too, but not much until April, when the friend of Delbecque's who headed the telephone-tapping branch was moved. The Minister for Algeria then promptly demanded Delbecque's removal, threatening to appeal to President Coty if necessary. He was not averse to protests from Algiers against the abandonment of his policy, and at first he had even encouraged the 26 April march; but now, fearing riots, he banned it. In contrast to September, however, the army leaders refused to enforce the ban. They were gratified by the complete orderliness of the marchers, who called for a Government of Public Safety (de Gaulle's name was still not mentioned). Delbecque (who had flown back to a military airfield which Lacoste did not control) seemed to have his following well in hand.

The demonstrators were to be bitterly disappointed. Gaillard had been overthrown to make way for a tougher policy with Tunisia; instead they were now told that a "sell-out government" was likely to come in. Bidault failed, Morice was blackballed, Pflimlin was proposed, Lacoste was to be evicted. Their indignation was fed by Lacoste himself, disgusted at his spineless party which was going to abandon him and his policy, and doubtless Algeria too. Publicly and privately he warned that a "diplomatic Dien Bien Phu" was being prepared. And on 8 May he bitterly attacked the generals for "civic cowardice" in refusing to make their real opinions known in Paris.

In this state of mind, Lacoste seemed a promising recruit for the men who were working to stop Pflimlin. Delbecque and Sérigny saw him on 9 May and urged him to lead the protest movement by announcing that he would remain at his post in Algiers until a Government of Public Safety took office. Delegations from the Vigilance Committee and Soustelle's organization USRAF were mobilized by Delbecque to reinforce his plea. The Minister hesitated, then refused. Next day he left for Paris, damned as a traitor by settler opinion. But he had not given up all hope that the *colons'* discontent might be a useful weapon against capitulation, for he is alleged to have told a Senator from Algiers "I hope you have a fine demonstration, and sack the town hall" (Mayor Jacques Chevallier—a Conservative, a Catholic and a Mendesist—was Lacoste's *bête noire*).

Delbecque, however, had no intention of using his demonstration to serve Lacoste's ends. His plan was to keep it going until the Assembly had voted. If Pflimlin won despite the protest, the crowd would invade the Ministry of Algeria (universally known as the *Gouvernement-Général* or GG) and the Vigilance Commitee would take over as a Committee of Public Safety. Soustelle was to fly in to lead the movement and issue an appeal to de Gaulle. And—it is said—paratroopers were to take off at once for Paris to support a simultaneous demonstration there. . . .

The Vigilance Committee had ordered a general strike for 1 p.m. on the 13th.

It was complete. Among the youths who soon filled the streets, leaflets circulated charging that Pflimlin would betray Algeria by negotiations in the summer, when the town was empty; Algiers must stop him now by insisting on a Government of Public Safety with Soustelle, Bidault, Morice and Duchet. The American Cultural Center was sacked by the crowd, but the offices of the *Journal d'Alger* (which supported Chevallier) were saved by paratroopers. At 5 p.m. a Vigilance Committee loudspeaker began whipping up feeling, denouncing the treacherous Paris politicians who were really responsible for the assassination of the murdered prisoners, repudiating any sell-out government, any government of the System, any authority except a Government of Public Safety. When the brief ceremony ended, at five past six, the generals went back to their headquarters and the crowd slowly started to disperse —both unaware that a revolution was taking place a few hundred yards away.

It was not Delbecque's revolution, of course; that was not due for hours. But neither was it Lagaillarde's and Martel's; their insurrection, too, was being stolen from under their noses. For the *lycéens*[8] of AGELCA had no intention of letting their seniors of AGEA monopolize the glory of the day. Well before the ceremony ended they were climbing the wide stairway which leads up from the War Memorial to the Forum, the big carpark in front of the GG. The CRS (riot police), who held the top, enraged them by using tear-gas. AGELCA loudspeakers below denounced this provocation, and the under-twenties swarmed to the attack on the hated police. Schoolboy messengers sped round the city on motorscooters to spread the word. At 6.5 p.m., as the generals left, Lagaillarde rather

---

[8] High school students.—Ed.

belatedly shouted, "Everyone to the GG to smash the rotten regime." The crowd on the steps grew. Suddenly someone— allegedly a paratroop colonel—ordered the CRS back into the building, leaving the Forum open. In the GG, Lacoste's *chef de cabinet* Maisonneuve was in charge. He phoned indignantly to the prefect (an ally of Delbecque's) and was told that parachutists were coming to take over. As none had come, Maisonneuve ordered the CRS to charge and clear the Forum; they did so, and he telephoned to Lacoste in Paris that it was all over. It had not yet begun.

The parachutists now arrived and occupied the top of the stairway, but did not stop the crowd invading the square (as one demonstrator put it, "they pushed us on while pretending to hold us back"). The *lycéens* started to wreck the parked cars of the GG officials who had not come out on strike. Senior officers appealed vainly (and quite inaudibly) for calm; Lacoste's military assistant Colonel Ducournau stood gesticulating impotently as his own car was turned over. At 6.15 p.m. about five hundred demonstrators began to attack the building. At one corner a few *lycéens* broke into the library and set it on fire. In front, the assailants stoned the CRS, who withdrew behind the gates. The paratroops let the attackers use one of their trucks as a battering-ram, and about 6.45 p.m. the gates gave way. . . .

As for Salan,[9] he had received a telephone appeal from the GG at 6.45 p.m., but hesitated some time before taking the subway from his HQ. He reached the GG soon after Massu, tried to address the crowd, and was howled down. Lagaillarde and the riot leaders urged Massu to head their Committee of Public Safety; at about 8.45 p.m., with no

guidance from Salan, he agreed in order (as he told a press conference next day) to keep them under control. At 9.10 p.m. he announced the CSP's[10] membership to the crowd: three paratroop colonels and four Moslems, suggested by the army, and seven rioters. None of these except Lagaillarde was known; one, asked whom he represented, replied proudly "The crowd." All proved to be ultras, not Gaullists. When Lacoste phoned from Paris to warn Massu of the dangers of his course, he was already committed. And when Delbecque at last arrived soon after nine o'clock, it seemed he had duly been robbed of his revolution. "I must admit we've got a bit ahead of your script," Lagaillarde remarked to him cheerfully. . . .

Delbecque at last reached the GG soon after 9 p.m., declared himself Soustelle's representative, optimistically announced his patron's imminent arrival, and was made vice-president of the CSP. After violent arguments several other Vigilance Committee members were also added. . . .

In Paris, readers of that morning's *Figaro* could have pondered an astonishingly accurate forecast of events by Serge Bromberger. Yet the politicians were taken completely by surprise. Deputies coming in one by one from dinner learned that the CSP had been formed, and were at once plunged into feverish excitement. But their reaction was not at all that hoped for by the demonstrators. Hesitant members, instead of voting against Pflimlin out of fear, rallied to him out of defiance. Without the demonstration against him, he would probably have lost; because of it he won comfortably, by 274 to 129. For the Communists decided to abstain. If they and their fellow-travellers had opposed

---

[9] Commander-in-Chief in Algeria, 1956-1958.—Ed.

[10] *Comité de Salut Public*—Committee of Public Safety.—Ed.

him, he would have had a majority of one.

His cabinet met in a mood of indignation, resolved to "smash the revolt" (Pierre de Chevigné, Minister of Defence), if necessary by "starving Algeria out" (Maurice Faure, Minister of the Interior). They brought gendarmerie reinforcements into Paris, put a police guard on Soustelle, and arrested some extreme-Right leaders and dissolved their parties. But with Algiers they were circumspect. Unanimously they decided to gamble that Salan and Massu were honest in claiming to have joined the revolt only to control it. Gaillard, as outgoing premier, had already delegated civil authority in Algiers to Salan, and Pflimlin confirmed this. . . .

But the ministers were wary, and they allowed their suspicions to show, Right-wingers were arrested in Paris, suspect generals were removed. The cabinet started to whittle away the authority it had granted to Salan, and tried to keep direct contact with loyal prefects. For over a week Algeria remained partially blockaded. The army concluded that the government's fair words were meant to lull them into passivity until ministers felt ready to pounce—and then, as one said, "it will rain close arrests." So the wily commander-in-chief [Salan], whose nickname was "the Chinese General," began cautiously to prepare an alternative line of action.

He was in an extraordinary position. For if the government seemed to have little confidence in him, the insurgents certainly had none. Delbecque and the Gaullists had been openly working for his replacement for months; and it was little more than a year since some of the ultras had tried to assassinate him. Most Europeans considered him "soft" and a time-server, and they had howled him down on the night of the 13th. And yet

no one wanted to offend him. The government needed his goodwill desperately. The ultras had cried *"L'armée au pouvoir!"* to frustrate Delbecque and de Gaulle, and the very existence of the CSP depended on the continued favour of the military. Delbecque himself also had to look to Salan, since Soustelle had failed him; if anyone was now to launch the appeal to de Gaulle, it must be the commander-in-chief. Thus everyone courted Salan, assuring him earnestly of their own friendship, and warning him amiably against the dark designs of their rivals.

So, when he spoke from the GG balcony for the second time, on the morning of Thursday the 15th, he was no longer friendless. It was an adroit speech, and the crowd cheered. In traditional style he ended, *"Vive l'Algérie française, vive la France!"* As he stepped back, Delbecque confronted him. Salan hesitated, then took a pace forward. *"Et vive de Gaulle!"*

For the handful of devoted Gaullists it was the decisive moment. In his concern for his own precarious position their enemy Salan had reopened the way to the solution which, on Tuesday night, had seemed blocked. But could they count on de Gaulle himself to play his part?

This had always been their greatest worry. Many who were not Gaullists had thought of the General in recent months: Presidents Coty and Bourguiba,[11] moderate nationalists from Algeria and Black Africa, liberal journalists and parliamentarians. For some Gaullists had been working hard and successfully to win support on the Left, and early in 1958 the General's keenest advocates were the left-wing critics of Mollet and Gaillard. But de Gaulle kept his silence. He had neither wanted nor expected the

[11] President of Tunisia.—Ed.

power which he would not take illegally, and saw no prospect of obtaining legally. In recent months, however, the many and varied public appeals to him, and the alarming news that the army was in "moral rebellion," had begun to influence his attitude. He neither approved nor even knew what Delbecque was planning. But he did tell the conspirator late in April, and confirm early in May, that if a crisis arose between Algeria and the homeland, he would at last speak out. So Delbecque had had his green light; and now the moment had come.

De Gaulle replied to Salan's appeal that same evening, with the concise statement, "I am ready to assume the powers of the Republic." There was jubilation in Algiers, and dismay on the Left. For the General's intervention changed everything. It staved off a possible collapse of the movement in Algeria. It also prevented a much more likely outcome: the seizure of power from the half-hearted Salan and the still uncommitted Massau by their impetuous and determined juniors, abetted by the ultras and eager to launch a military invasion of the mainland. But de Gaulle's statement had positive effects too. In the army in France, in the administration, and among the Algerian Moslems themselves it won for the movement a sympathy which no one else could have commanded.

To the army and the Right, de Gaulle's name stood for inflexible patriotism: he was a guarantee against a sell-out. But for many on the Left he was also the man who had restored democracy fourteen years before: a safeguard against fascism. Reassuring both sides, he was the solution which divided Frenchmen least, and the best hope of averting civil war. . . .

The General entered the Palais d'Orsay punctually at 3 p.m. [for his press conference]. His performance was most skillful. He wooed the Socialists, referring by name to "my friend" Lacoste and Mollet "whom I esteem" (and to no one else), reminding them of the socialistic achievements of his previous ministry, and repudiating as absurd the idea that he would ever overturn the liberties he had himself restored. But he also praised the intervention of the army, refused to condemn the Algiers leaders, and urged the Assembly to adopt a special procedure for his legal accession to power. So carefully did he hold the balance that both sides were dissatisfied, and opinion in Algiers was ready to condemn the "compromiser"—until the moment when the Socialists denounced his factious and unconstitutional conduct, whereupon he again found grace across the Mediterranean.

Now for a moment there seemed to be a lull in the storm. The Communist general strike, called for the moment when de Gaulle was to speak, was an utter failure—like the abortive demonstrations which Biaggi[12] and the friends of Algiers had planned for the evening of 13 May. The cabinet made no reply to de Gaulle's press conference. Behind the scenes, however, there was frantic activity: Gaullists and right-wingers preparing an insurrectionary movement in France; soldiers in Algiers perfecting plans for an invasion of the mainland; politicians exploring ways to avert honourably a disastrous civil war. Colombey-les-deux-Eglises began to receive distinguished visitors. Pinay (no Gaullist) went on Thursday the 22nd, after seeing Pflimlin the day before; he returned enthusiastic for the General. Piette, a Socialist deputy and friend of Mollet, followed on Friday; *Personne y était"* said the critics when Mollet denied meeting de Gaulle, for in the Resistance Piette had been called "Colonel Per-

[12] Right-wing agitator.—Ed.

sonne." But at the weekend the slow-motion reel was suddenly speeded up. Algiers precipitated matters by the seizure of Corsica.

This step was decisive. The army leaders knew they had gone too far to retreat; if Pflimlin survived, they were ruined. Massu had already drawn up a 32-page plan for the airborne invasion of the mainland. But the wily Salan would not commit himself so far; a peaceful demonstration in Corsica seemed a far safer alternative. So Massu and Delbecque persuaded him to authorize an action which—whether he intended it or not—was to snap his frail link to Paris. For the expedition became an open challenge to the government. . . .

The French state had been withering away for years. Now the process reached its climax. "You are not abandoning power," a left-wing Gaullist told ministers in the Assembly. "It has abandoned you." The civil service, on Moch's[13] evidence, offered "inert opposition" to cabinet decisions. In his own Ministry, once the Republic's holy of holies, officials concealed information from him—or gleefully supplied it, when it seemed likely to intimidate ministers by revealing the extent of the conspiracy. The police in the capital had shown their sympathies sufficiently by their ugly demonstration in March; the gendarmerie (who came under the Ministry of Defence) shared the outlook of the army; even the firemen, so useful in riots, were disaffected—as their colonel put it, they would stick to their job of putting out fires—"but if the Palais Bourbon caught alight, I doubt if they'd bother." Moch's own creation, the CRS, neither could nor would fight the army. He thought half of them loyal, and entrusted the defence of Paris to them—but the conspirators

[13] Minister of the Interior.—Ed.

were convinced that these same CRS were panting with eagerness to join the revolt, and they planned to take over the capital with the very forces which the government had collected to defend it.

The navy was more or less "neutralist." But the air force was brazen. Openly, its planes traversed the skies in Cross of Lorraine formation; covertly, its commanders flew across to Algeria the troop-carrying planes necessary for an invasion of the mainland. The army was seething. . . .

At the last meeting of the Pflimlin cabinet, Pleven summed matters up. "We are the legal government. But what do we govern? The Minister for Algeria cannot enter Algeria. The Minister for the Sahara cannot go to the Sahara. The Minister of Information can do nothing but censor the press. The Minister of the Interior has no control over the police. The Minister of Defence is disobeyed by the army."

Some ministers were still prepared for a final throw: to move the seat of government to the 'red bastion' of the northern coalfield, on the Belgian border, and arm the miners. Mollet spoke romantically of dying among them on the barricades. But would they have marched? On 19 May only 800 of the 300,000 Nord miners had struck; in the Renault works near Paris, 3 per cent had come out. The Nord responded well to another strike call on the 27th; but in Paris it was a pathetic failure. Not even Communists would strike (or indeed always vote, as the referendum later showed) against de Gaulle. Certainly they were unwilling as well as unable to fight against him. The demonstrators who marched from the Place de la Nation to the Place de la République on 28 May were indeed impressively numerous (200–250,000 by the highest Gaullist and lowest anti-Gaullist estimates). But they were hardly the vanguard of a civil war army: and a few ribald slogans like *"De Gaulle au musée!"* and *"La girafe au zoo!"* mingled with *"Vive la République!,"* *"Front populaire!"* and *"Le fascime ne passera pas!"* Yet the very suggestion of a Popular Front was self-defeating, for it would have alienated the rest of the nation, and shattered in pieces the cabinet itself. "It would have been the war in Spain," remarked Mollet—"but without the Republican army." And Moch advised wryly, "Always avoid a civil war—especially when you are sure to lose". . . .

Moch's emotion on hearing the news of de Gaulle's announcement that he had "begun the regular process of forming a republican government" was not indignation but profound relief; de Gaulle, then, was not in the conspiracy but was trying to stop it. For at 10 a.m. Moch had learned from a diplomatic source (apparently the American Consul at Algiers) that the invasion of the mainland was to be launched that night. "Operation Resurrection" would be commanded by General Miquel under orders from Algiers. Tanks from the Paris garrison were to seize Le Bourget and Villacoublay airfields; Miquel's parachutists from the south-west would begin to land at 2.30 a.m., those from Algiers at 5.30 a.m. But most of the "paratroops" who were to take over Paris would be recalled reservists, Indo-China veterans—and the police and CRS whom the government expected to oppose them. All would wear parachutist uniforms. Prefectures throughout the south would be occupied by the CSP's which were waiting in the wings, while the army stood by benevolently to "preserve order." If the government fled northwards, it would be cut off by the troops in Germany under General Jacques Faure, hero of an earlier and abortive conspiracy.

All the generals fervently hoped to win by threats alone. Beaufort, who was to command in Paris, personally told the Elysée just what was planned, and when. But this does not mean they (still less their subordinates) were merely bluffing. Moch, the strong man of the government, never believed so. He was convinced that an irretrievable calamity was imminent, and that de Gaulle had shown his good faith by intervening to stop it—thus keeping open the legal road to power which alone he was ready to take.

Moch was right in his assumption, and Algiers did postpone the attack. But in parliament, among less informed or more incredulous deputies, resistance to de Gaulle stiffened when his extraordinary communiqué became known. The Socialists voted overwhelmingly (117 to 3) never to accept him, MRP urged Pflimlin to stay in office. The Conservatives indeed ordered their ministers to resign (one refused). But a large majority of the Assembly was striving—for once—not to throw out a reluctant cabinet but to keep one in. A constitutional reform bill (proposed in the vain hope of taking the wind out of de Gaulle's sails) passed by 408 to 165: no pretext there for resignation. The Socialist Ministers urged Pflimlin to stay—not to block de Gaulle, but to give time to work on their party, for they feared a vote that day meant a Popular Front under Mitterrand. But the Premier was determined, and at 4 a.m. on Wednesday the 28th he resigned (after receiving more frequent and comfortable votes of confidence than any of his predecessors could boast).

To choose a successor was the task of the President of the Republic, René Coty, a respectable conservative surrounded by ardent (though sometimes recent) Gaullists. In the afternoon, as the republican demonstrators were gathering in eastern Paris, he told the party leaders that the choice was de Gaulle or a Popular Front, and he would do his utmost for the former. At midnight the General came once again to St. Cloud to meet Coty's representatives, the Presidents of the two houses: for the deputies André Le Troquer, a one-armed Socialist, and for the senators Gaston Monnerville, a coloured Radical; ex-President Vincent Auriol had declined. The meeting was not a success. Twelve years before, de Gaulle had sworn he would never set foot in the Assembly again; Le Troquer insisted he must come to make the customary speech before his election. The General wanted exceptional powers for two years. "Three months" offered Le Troquer. "Six" was Monnerville's pacific contribution. Moreover, de Gaulle demanded the right to draft a new constitution; Le Troquer would not hear of it. At 1 a.m. they parted angrily. The crisis was at its peak.

Algiers resumed its invasion plans— for the coming night, Thursday 29 May. Le Troquer spread gloom among his Socialist colleagues at their morning meeting; Moch instructed prefects to take to the *maquis* if necessary. At 3 p.m. the deputies met to hear their own President read the first and last special message from a President of the Fourth Republic. Only de Gaulle could avert civil war, declared Coty; if the Assembly rejected him, he would himself resign.

Constitutionally, his powers would then pass to the President of the Assembly. . . .

Next afternoon de Gaulle met the party leaders, twenty-six of them, at the Hôtel Lapérouse (the Communists were invited, but refused). He agreed after all to appear before the Assembly, but he would not answer questions (he cited a sound precedent, set by Joseph Laniel, perhaps the least distinguished and successful of the Fourth Republic's fifteen premiers). He revealed the outline of his constitutional plans. There were a few questions, mostly about his attitude to the Committees of Public Safety. That night Gaullists and Communists clashed on the Champs Elysées, the police openly taking sides; and at Toulouse General Miquel, the prospective commander of Operation Resurrection, withstood pressure to launch the invasion after all, for some extremists were bent on averting any compromise with the hated System. At 3 p.m. on Sunday de Gaulle entered the Assembly to read the shortest investiture speech of the Fourth Republic, then withdrew for the brief debate. The house voted at twenty-five minutes to eight. Among the General's 329 supporters were forty-two Socialists; among his 224 opponents, forty-nine. Three weeks earlier he would not have had fifty votes. Georges Bidault remarked that his speech might well have been shorter still: "Gentleman, between you and the Seine is—me."

LEO HAMON (1907–   ), an Appeal Court lawyer, vice-president of the Parisian Liberation Committee during the Resistance and senator for the Seine department since 1946, was excluded from the MRP for his opposition to European integration. A self-styled "Gaullist of the Left," he holds that the circumstances of de Gaulle's return to power are a side issue. Taking up the arguments and even the style Cattaui used in defense of de Gaulle's break with Pétain, he argues that a "crystallization around de Gaulle" took place because he represented the French people's wish for greatness, national unity and effective government. He also, however, claims, as Aron did at the time of the RPF, that de Gaulle stood, not for the maintenance of out-of-date institutions, but for the modernization of French society.*

Symbol of Greatness and National Unity

The regime thus fell victim to its own contradictions, to its "essential absurdity" which was obvious to everyone except its rulers. The "Algiers coup"— whether plot or revolution, call it what one will—is certainly worth study and reflection; but those who concentrate their political efforts on it, to denounce and criticize it, are dealing only with a side issue, not with the principal one. Anger in someone with high blood pressure is a cause of death, but it is because of his own excessive tensions that he perishes. "The Fourth Republic died much less because of the blows it received," Sirius concluded, "than from its own inability to go on living." If the political regime had been "satisfactory,"

the Algiers plot would have failed; better yet, it would probably not have existed.

The French problem would thus have been posed if General de Gaulle had not been there. Imagine that he had died on his last trip through the French Union, or on one of his last trips from Colombey to Paris. Does anyone believe that, as a result, the contradictions within the regime would have been less and its survival any longer? It would be all the more unreasonable to assume it, since in fact, up to May 13 [1958] General de Gaulle had been above all a witness, a spectator.

To seize power, both Napoleons acted; since the end of the RPF, what has been

* From Léo Hamon, *De Gaulle dans la République* (Paris: Librairie Plon, 1958), pp. 46–47, 49–54, 63–64, 66–68. Translated by editor. Footnotes omitted.

the activity of General de Gaulle? Those who wished for his return had vainly demanded, for many long months, that he speak and express by his voice the sufferings of the nation. Common Market, installation of foreign launching pads, affairs in the Maghreb, federal union—we would have liked him to take a position on these subjects; he refused, saying that his words would be distorted. He no longer had a party; never was a man more alone, apart from a few faithful. The popular phrase is true; they "went to find him." To those who wanted his return, he replied that it was unthinkable; did not he himself believe that?

Rarely has a movement been so spontaneous; in a few weeks it was on him that the will for a French revival crystallized. Why? In what sense? How could a name succeed in imposing itself in so little time with, at the start, so little force of its own? There is subject matter here for instructive sociological research. Let us try to anticipate it a little. . . .

The will for greatness, the affirmation of a nation's wish to live, the need, in order to escape from discredited political alliances, of someone who had never belonged to them, and finally the longing for national unity—these were without doubt the decisive factors, of which people were more or less aware, in the movement that turned toward General de Gaulle.

Those who knew him, or had even been near him, were aware of his religion of *French greatness*; more numerous were those who remembered the *intransigence* with which he had always affirmed the rights of France during the war not only against the invaders but even against the encroachments of our allies themselves, and later against American pre-

dominance, Communist "separatism," and "European disintegration." They perhaps remembered no more than this constant theme: "He, at least, always thinks French; with him we shall not be humiliated."

For the most worried, for the most humble, he was the symbol of the last great French victory: the Liberation. Perhaps, unlike us, they had not wept on seeing him again on France's soil; perhaps they had forgotten the details of his actions and his words from that London radio whose waves braved the powerful armory of Goliath and predicted the victory of David . . . which was achieved. The choice of the V[1] was significant: it was indeed the victory of which France was speaking . . . and France once again felt the need to talk of it.

The most recent affirmation of our will to live, our victory and our pride—de Gaulle had embodied all that gave each Frenchman reason to be proud of himself, and as a result he felt taller, even if he had not taken an active personal role. As a result, the epic struggle did for de Gaulle what birth had done previously for the heir to the throne; he was the living House of France. When, exhausted with humiliation, Frenchmen felt the need to be proud, they naturally had to turn to him.

Thus the army's decision, for the most part, can be explained. Tested by two wars overseas, humiliated in the first, worried about the second, it wanted, more than any particular policy, the certainty that its honor would be guaranteed.

It could take the risk of political differences, the risk of seeing imposed upon

---

[1] The Morse signal ···—, V for Victory, was used by the BBC to introduce its broadcasts to Occupied Europe.—Ed.

itself a choice it disagreed with—if it had the certainty that the government would not accept defeat; and did not General de Gaulle enter history by refusing defeat?

Among the Europeans in Algeria themselves, the defense of privilege and racism could be mixed with the pride of being French and the fear of being abandoned —these latter feelings existed no less than the former. De Gaulle was, for them, the assurance that with him French pride would be in power and that abandonment would not be the program of the day.

That this movement should have become suddenly so powerful and irresistible, that in less than three weeks it should have brought to power one whose sole strength was to represent French greatness, is a fact; and it shows how much the pride of men is linked with their national consciousness, how sovereign are the commands of that consciousness at certain moments. . . .

The need for national unity was another essential consideration. Between resolute minorities, ready to fight for their respective theses—Republican defense or "new order"—a majority of French people wanted peace above all. "What we want most of all is not such or such a result but it is that this should end without a struggle"—who has not heard that said during these days? The desire for public peace is perhaps the least high form of anxiety for national unity, but is it not also the sense, more or less vague, of the need for union imposing an end to discord?

Well, who could divide us the least while exalting us the most? Here again the reply was: de Gaulle. He was a guarantee for the army. Who could impugn his patriotism, who on the Right could present him as a self-seeker or a crypto-

Communist? For the democrats, he was also a guarantee. Who indeed on the Left could successfully present him as a fascist?

The Communist party tried, it is true; the lack of response was significant. Any other than de Gaulle, acclaimed by Algiers, desired by the army, would have had all republicans against him, and would have been strongly opposed as a consequence. With him, because of the Resistance and the Liberation, "it was something quite different." "We're not afraid of him but of those who are behind him," a Parisian workman, doubtless a Communist voter, said to me in the last days of May. With anyone else enjoying, let us suppose, the same military support, the end result would probably have been the same; but, however brief, civil war would have tainted the new authority. We could not have brought it the active support of the Left and its forces; at least nobody could deprive him of the neutrality of the forces of the Left. . . . So, at the same time that he was the symbol of our national pride, he was recognized as the sign of our unity, and we were grateful to him for that, the more we worried about knowing so little the aims of others. . . .

The third reason for the crystallization around de Gaulle was his position outside the parties. For ten years, France was governed by party men. To participate in public affairs, it was necessary to have the stamp of approval of one of the parties. The membership card had replaced the shield of nobility. But the choices presented by the existing parties appeared at first ineffective and then meaningless to an increasing number of Frenchmen—and the divisions and fragmentation they were condemned to seemed foolish. People wanted to choose worthwhile men from this party or from that; the temptation to split one's vote, so often felt by the elector, was proof of his discomfort at being confronted with choices he did not wish to make . . . choices that he was not wrong in considering morally fallacious. The fierce opposition of the parties and their true similarity of attitude was irritating, as was the place given to abusive behavior.

Was it necessary in order "to vote Mendès-France" to give one's ballot to M. Bourgès-Maunoury, or to get "peace in Algeria" to vote for whoever was demanding the repeal of the *Loi Barangé*?[2] The identification of persons and party programs seemed at once arbitrary, irritating, and artificial.

Finally, public opinion recognized instinctively in the parties the entangling web of a system that it had come to condemn and to despise. It felt that these parties, once capable of action and achievement, had been immobilized by their entanglement. Nevertheless, talking incessantly and forever holding the front of the stage, they identified themselves with what it was necessary to abolish . . . without, for all that, increasing our freedom, the taste for which is so strong in our people.

In this last regard, it has been pointed out, a general without any political experience or an agitator of any kind would not have been able to settle the affair; they would have promised order but would have caused fears for our freedom. Someone who was democratic without being partisan, illustrious without being effaced by the parties' investiture or support, was thus required; it was not at all easy to find him. To a nation that felt itself imprisoned within the walls of the political parties, which were piled one on the other like so many stones,

[2] Law passed in 1951 giving state aid to parochial schools.—Ed.

Charles de Gaulle appeared to be a tall chimney bringing pure air.

To whoever asked him, during the past year, to take a position and when he refused still insisted, he replied, ironically if not bitterly, "Through my silence, I shall become a new man. . . ." "As in 1940," he might have added. His fate will have been, in fact, to have been chosen twice as a "new man," when the nation had been abandoned by its old, or had turned against them. . . .

There were other supporters of de Gaulle's return: the upper ranks of the administration, civil servants who saw in him the personification of the requirements of the State above the parties whose disputes might well appear to them derisory and irritating at the same time. They were not "technocrats," with all that the word implies of attachment to an isolated class, of ignorance of popular desires and of social concerns. They were rather an aristocracy of state servants; many, who had arisen in the Resistance, had remained bound to it by their memories of that heroic epoch. Entering public life at the Liberation, in the service of the nation and of the republic, they had the good fortune to begin their careers "at the level of the highest ideals," and the subsequent need to choose between the parties, none of which was up to the level of their dreams or of their first aspirations, wearied them; France remained their lady. Was not Charles de Gaulle her avowed paladin? They also refused to be diverted from her service by disputes that lacked greatness.

They liked de Gaulle's talent for decision and for action, which is inseparable from an effective administration. To tell the truth, they no longer believed that his return to power was possible. Two or three years ago, we were discussing the best form of government . . . or the least bad. It was, I still remember, at Granada on the terrace of the Alhambra, and so much exotic past beauty made us wish even more to see the present of our country more beautiful. I asked my companion, "And de Gaulle?" He replied, "That would be too fine, but it is not possible." More exactly, he was doubtless thinking, "It would not be possible except through a *coup d'état* and a Rightist movement," which both his reason and his heart opposed. And yet what if, without the state's collapsing, service of the republic could again become an admirable way of life—and regain its primacy?

In this way was formed the outline of a *third Gaullism* (the first being the Resistance and the second the RPF).

More or less consciously, for some, it represented the affirmation of the supremacy of national values, the desire for French greatness and for an independent French policy, less involved in the East-West quarrel, for a state finally effective enough to preside over the modernization of our country, over a social and overseas evolution that could be rapid without becoming uncontrolled (or controlled by others)—the desire that one's country and the republic should be in touch with reality in order to act in accordance with reality; and this, *omisso medio,* by rising above party quarrels whose policies and divisions appeared each time to us to be destroying our love for our country. . . .

Thus, through this Gaullism and in it a group of men drew up their conception of their form of government: what has been called the "the power élites," and more generally all those, state officials or others, whose thinking had been formed by reflection on the needs of the state and of the nation. The role of satisfying these needs was more and more, as a result of the "jamming" of the parties, left vacant; they proposed de Gaulle and through him proposed themselves for that role, not against the parties but by the side of them and without being exclusively dependent upon them.

They were a social class whose importance had grown with the functions of the State. More numerous and more influential, they naturally carried more weight. Their idea of government corresponds to something which, in a modern State, is not at all negligible and which comprises one of the possible solutions to the problems of the present. Is it viable in reality? We shall have to return to that (events above all will decide); but the very attempt would have no chance to be recognized and accepted without the personality and the signal of General de Gaulle.

In him, the *knights of the state* became conscious of their community; through him, their chivalry could speak to the crowds, even make itself popular and become a factor in politics. Even with him, the success of a government of this type would be a new experience; but without him, the formation of a government of this type would have remained a chimera. . . . Such is, and remains, the third Gaullism.

De Gaulle's treatment of the Algerian problem throws much light on his character as a statesman. It required four more years of war, marked by uprisings of European settlers and the French army and culminating in terrorism, attempts on de Gaulle's life, and the flight of the major part of the European population, before Algeria gained its independence. One must ask whether this long delay was due to de Gaulle's need to win over the French people to a far-sighted solution that he had already envisaged in 1958, to his unwillingness to give up the most important remnant of France's colonial empire, or to his slow empirical search for a solution that would be workable. In this extract from his biography of de Gaulle, PAUL-MARIE DE LA GORCE (1925–   ), a French journalist and author of a history of the French army, portrays de Gaulle as a pragmatist whose thinking evolved under the pressure of events.*

▶ *Algerian Vicissitudes*

Between May 13 and June 1 de Gaulle published three communiqués, held a press conference, gave his "investiture" speech, wrote two letters that were made public, and had several conversations which were widely publicized. Not once did he indicate precisely his views on the future of Algeria; for even better reasons, he never spoke of "French Algeria" or of "integration." This silence promised future crises. For the moment, it justified the most diverse and the most contradictory speculation. Moreover, ambiguous opinions had been conceived already. Shorty after May 13, Michel Debré[1] had been put in contact, by

[1] Minister of Justice, 1958; Premier, 1959–1962.—Ed.

the head of the Arabic services of Algiers-Radio, with two of the principal leaders of the FLN in Algeria. Their talk took place on a farm in the outskirts of Algiers; they dined and their conversation was cordial. Speaking of the future of Algeria, Neuwirth said that it should be "linked to France," and spoke of a "French framework," avoiding using the word integration. Above all, he insisted on the opposition between the Gaullists and the activists, repudiating the latter's "fascism" and racism. It is not impossible that this discussion might have brought about, to some extent, the neutrality that the FLN observed in all the towns of Algeria—and which was, in practice, favorable to the movement of

* From Paul-Marie de la Gorce, *De Gaulle entre deux mondes: Une Vie et une époque* (Paris: Librairie Arthème Fayard, 1964), pp. 613–616, 618–620, 623–627, 630–635, 637–640, 643–646, 648–650, 652, 661–662, 665–666. Translated by editor.

May 13. One can see in it, in any case, the distant beginning of the complex game that was to bring into conflict de Gaulle, Algerian nationalism, the French army, and the European community. . . .

On the fifth [of June], Delbecque disclosed that the struggle begun on May 13 was not over: "We didn't cross the Rubicon to go fishing." De Gaulle at once made clear that he would not be moved by the pressure of his former companions. Already on June 1, on coming to Paris, Delbecque had felt the distance that separated the Algiers movement from the state of mind of the men who surrounded de Gaulle, especially of Georges Pompidou and Olivier Guichard, the director and assistant director of his staff. He had even noticed some uncertainty in Lucian Neuwirth,[2] who he had thought, nevertheless, would be an intransigent supporter of French Algeria.

On June 6, in Oran, de Gaulle began by refusing to see the town's Committee of Public Safety. It required strong pressure to make him change his decision. . . . No one doubted, in European circles, that he was already envisaging the liquidation of the Committees of Public Safety. In vain did the crowd at Mostaganem that afternoon hear him shout, "Long live Mostaganem! Long live French Algeria! Long live the Republic! Long live France!" It was the only time he spoke of "French Algeria." But the political climate in Algiers was not changed by it; on the radio, everyone heard him shout, "Be quiet," to demonstrators who were cheering Soustelle. After June 7, the leaders of the activist movements and of the European organizations sought to reply.

Their reply came two days later. The "Algiers-Sahara" Committee of Public

Safety voted a motion demanding "the disappearance of all administrative organizations indicating Algerian particularism" but also the "suppression of the political parties." Salan passed it on to de Gaulle. Immediately, de Gaulle replied:

With regard to the annoying and untimely incident caused by the peremptory motion of the Algiers Committee of Public Safety, I remind you that this committee has no other right and role than to express, under your supervision, the opinion of its members. The regular authorities, and you yourself first of all, may not decide to support what this committee or any other political organization should express or demand.

Scarcely a week had passed since de Gaulle had taken power; already the divorce was in sight. Soon the extreme elements of the "Algiers-Sahara" Committee of Public Safety would resign and pass openly into the opposition. . . .

For two months, de Gaulle had not stopped affirming the French character, not of Algeria, but of all Algerians. From "ten million full-share Frenchmen" to "absolute equality of rights and duties," a long series of phrases took up the same idea. In that way, the European minority was denied any superiority. But in that way also "Algerianity" seemed to be refused to the Algerians, who saw themselves proclaimed to be French citizens. If Algeria itself were to be bound to France, at once integration would be assured and accomplished; but if this link were neither absolute nor definitive, the destiny of Algeria would be that desired by the Algerians, that is to say, by the overwhelming Moslem majority of the population. This ambiguity hid the choice between two policies that were radically opposite, and that is why it aroused the growing exasperation of the supporters of "French Algeria."

[2] Gaullist leader in Algerian uprising of May 13, 1958.—Ed.

Ending his African tour at Dakar, de Gaulle had confided to Gabriel d'Arboussier,[3] "It is for Algeria that I am constructing the Community." Thus, Algeria would be promised the autonomous future reserved for the States of the Community, but it would be within a French framework, wider than France— that was his expression in 1955. The success of the Community would convince the Algerians of the immense future that it offered to them; in this "French framework" the Europeans would have nothing to fear. A little later, de Gaulle was to assure the leading citizens of Rennes, "Independence is impossible, and so is integration in the form in which it is proposed."

It was still necessary to make the Algerians themselves understand. On August 28, he made it clear to a group whom he received secretly in Algiers. Then he recorded the speech that was to be broadcast the next day, one paragraph of which defined the political significance of the referendum [on the new French constitution]:

The inhabitants of Algeria are going to reply to the question of their own future by their vote. For however hard the trials of a fratricidal war are, whatever the idea that one group or another may have of what the future status of their country should be, once peace has returned and the disturbances passed, the ballots that they will put in the urn will have a clear meaning on one capital point. For everyone to reply "Yes!" in the present circumstances will mean at the very least that you wish to behave as full-share French citizens and that you wish the necessary evolution of Algeria to be completed within the French framework.

In this paragraph, "French framework" left several paths open, while the ex-pression "full-share Frenchmen" still reflected the spirit of May 13; but by appealing to all Algerians "whatever the idea that one group or another may have of what the future status of their country should be," de Gaulle expressly pointed out that several solutions were still possible. On the spot, in fact, the powerful civil and military administration—in existence before May 13 but largely consolidated and reinforced since —completely identified the "Yes" vote with the success of French Algeria. De Gaulle wanted to change the orientation of the official propaganda; a series of meetings was held in Algiers in which Bernard Tricot[4] was ordered to describe —or impose—de Gaulle's directives. In practice, the controversy was so fundamental that it could not be solved other than by a major crisis. A few days before the ballot, set for September 28, de Gaulle was staking his personal authority, his general policy, the reform of the State, and the future of French Africa. In Algeria, the strength of the army, of the administration, and of the political movements that arose out of the 13th of May was exercised without hesitation. The result was one that could have been expected; 96 percent voted "Yes."

To all appearances, the supporters of French Algeria were going to be more self-assured than ever. By putting their mark on all the referendum campaign, they had given the vote a different meaning from the one de Gaulle had wanted. He was all the more irritated at this since he had firmly decided to reject "integration in the form in which it is proposed." A few days earlier he had said so straight out to Félix Gaillard, who had just been elected president of the Radical party. He therefore had to act.

[3] President of the Grand Council of French West Africa.—Ed.

[4] Member of de Gaulle's staff.—Ed.

On October 3, he was at Constantine. After a long enumeration of the economic and social reforms that were to be carried out during the next five years, he devoted several sentences to the political future:

This profound evolution, where can it lead? As to the political status of Algeria, I believe it quite useless to congeal in advance in words the shape that the enterprise will take little by little. But in any case, two things are certain now. The first concerns the present. In two months, Algeria will elect its representatives under the same conditions as the mainland itself. But two-thirds of the representatives will have to be Moslem citizens. The other matter concerns the future. The future of Algeria, at any rate— because that is the nature of things—will be built on a double base: its personality and its close solidarity with the French mainland.

Four months after his return to power, de Gaulle was revealing the basis of what would be, henceforth, his Algerian policy: it would be evolutionary and empirical since it was a question of moving into a future that "the enterprise will shape little by little"; and it would apparently be neither integration nor total independence, since "the personality" of Algeria and its "close solidarity with France" were in some way on the same footing. . . .

This new current reached its culmination on October 23. That day de Gaulle held his first press conference since his return to power. The passage that he was to devote to Algeria was awaited passionately.

I say unequivocally that for the most part the men in the insurrection have fought courageously. Let the peace of the brave come and I am sure that the hatreds will be wiped out. I have spoken of the peace of the brave. What does that mean? Simply this: that those who opened fire should cease fire and that they should return without

humiliation to their families and to their work! You say to me: "But how can they arrange the end of the fighting?" I reply: there, where they are organized for battle, their leaders have only to contact the army command. The old wisdom of the warrior has, for a very long time, used the parliamentarians' white flag when one wanted the weapons to become silent. And I reply that in that case the soldiers would be received and treated honorably. As to the outside organization of which we were just speaking [the FLN] which is attempting to direct the struggle from abroad, I reply openly what I have already made known. If delegates were named to come to settle the end of hostilities with the authorities, they have only to make contact with the French embassy in Tunis or at Rabat. One or the other would provide their transport to the mainland. There, complete safety would be assured them, and I guarantee their freedom to leave.

But on the 25th the FLN declared that it would only accept military and political negotiations held in a neutral country, cutting short speculations or hopes that had been born. And in November, without any candidates who were liberal or simply favorable to autonomy being named, the general elections brought about total victory in Algeria for the supporters of integration. . . . From all the evidence, the Algerian policy of the government was in a kind of impasse; the elections had not brought forward that "political élite" whose birth de Gaulle had wished for. In any case, nothing gave further hope that peace would be restored quickly.

De Gaulle was struck to the quick by the refusal of his offers of a "peace of the brave." The FLN's refusal seemed to him a mark of distrust toward him, but also, and above all, a lack of clear-sightedness on its part.

From that moment, he had a mediocre opinion of the leaders of the Algerian insurrection. He had the tendency to believe that they were incapable of accepting political risks and unable to perceive the opportunities for Algeria in a wider, more modern grouping. Not without a certain silent exasperation he saw them withdrawing into an intransigence that was easier for them and at the same time more costly for their people. It was thus, at least, that he considered their decision to continue the struggle and that he judged the combat methods chosen by the FLN. . . . After the October experience, it seemed to him that only the steady application of his Algerian policy would end by winning the support of a large proportion of the Moslems and would one day force the FLN to change its attitude. As a result, all negotiations were barred. . . .

Nevertheless, at the end of the spring [of 1959], de Gaulle was sensitive to the immobility that seemed to paralyze all political life in Algeria. He had vainly denounced "papa's Algeria" in an interview with Pierre Laffont, director of *L'Echo d'Oran*: the municipal elections proved that the supremacy of the European community remained complete in fact and that the Moslem masses remained withdrawn. Despite the intervention of the civilian administration, the Moslems elected were almost always those whose candidature had been instigated by the officers. No sign of relaxation or of evolution was in sight. . . . It was necessary to cause a shock whose impact would stir the Moslem population and gain the support at the same time of world and French opinion.

De Gaulle attached immense importance to preparing his new proposal in such a way as to give it a certain solemnity. . . . Even in form and tone the speech of September 16 [1959] aimed to achieve the greatest effect. A sentence of a certain official majesty summarized its spirit:

In the name of France and of the Republic, in virtue of the power invested in me by the Constitution of consulting the citizens, providing that God gives me life and that the people hear me, I undertake to ask, on the one side, the Algerians in their twelve departments, what they definitively wish to be, and on the other side, to ask all French people to ratify that choice.

To recognize Algeria's right to self-determination was to give a new and spectacular form to the idea expressed often, but in vague terms, since the previous year. But it was, above all, opening the way to the separation of France and Algeria. From then on, in fact, the Algerian departments were no longer part of the indivisible republic. They could choose another destiny and form a new State. In itself, the speech of September 16 went part of the way that was to lead to the independence of Algeria. It swept away, with one blow, a series of political and juridical obstacles that it would have been necessary, regardless, to overcome. In advance, the ground for eventual negotiations with the adversary was defined; they would concern the conditions of self-determination but also perhaps the content of the choices offered to the Algerians.

De Gaulle had foreseen three: secession, Francization, and association. The first was described in such terms that de Gaulle evidently excluded it: "Algeria being what it is today and the world being what we know it to be, secession would bring frightful misery, terrible political chaos, and, soon, the warlike dictatorship of the Communists. . . ." Nothing made apparent, to be precise, his opinion on Francization; the most he did was to describe it in such a way as to make people understand all the economic, social, and psychological implications. By being described last, the solution of association seemed to be the one desired by de Gaulle, especially as one saw again there the mark of his earlier proposals. This time he gave a more complete definition:

Government of the Algerians by the Algerians, supported with the aid of France and in close union with it, for the economy, education, defense, and foreign affairs. In that case, the internal regime of Algeria should be of a federal type, so that the different communities, French, Arab, Kabyle, Mazabite, etc., who live together in the country, should find there guarantees for their own life and a framework for their cooperation.

The last part of the speech was addressed to the FLN. Once again, it was invited to put an end to the struggle, but this time de Gaulle expressly envisaged its future role in Algerian political life.... Yet he expressed clearly his intention of not recognizing it as the exclusive representative of the Algerian people. Even more, he denounced its members in advance as usurpers and dictators, should they refuse to play the game of self-determination....

It was then that the FLN officially designated its five leaders—Ben Bella, Boudiaf, Ait Ahmed, Khidder, and Rabah Bitat—who had been arrested in 1956, to open conversations. Reasons related to the internal problems of the FLN had doubtless governed this choice; in any case, one could not believe that men who had been imprisoned for two years could effectively negotiate on the conditions of a cease-fire. De Gaulle held the decision of the FLN to be a disguised, and almost rude, refusal. At once all the hopes for an early end to the war disappeared. Personally, he saw in it the confirmation of his pessimistic judgment on the intentions and attitude of the FLN. From then on, there remained only the patient search—vain until then—for the "political élite" whose appearance he had awaited for more than a year....

It was only little by little, and not without irritation, that [de Gaulle] perceived the new traits of the French army. The army was abandoning itself completely to that current whose violence May 13 had revealed. As a whole it appeared, henceforth, as a tight intellectual and social structure. All its hierarchies were adopting officially the conceptions defended until then by only a few officers on the idea of subversive war and on the consequences that the French army should draw from them. Henceforth, in the general staffs, at the War School, in the speeches to the troops, they repeated indefatigably that the decisive factor in future war is the "attitude of the populations." They deduced from this that the army should have recourse to all the techniques suitable for giving it control of that attitude.... And certainly, the assimilation of Algerian nationalism to international communism, the first being only the "waiting room" for the second, took the importance of a dogma. It was the West that France was defending in Algeria against the FLN. It would henceforth be a heresy to claim the contrary.... Thus, from the summer of 1958, de Gaulle's refusal of open integration aroused in the army a deep worry. This grew still further as de Gaulle spoke more frequently of the Algerian personality or declared that "all opinions" could be expressed and contribute to defining the future status of Algeria.... For many in the army, a lasting incomprehension existed between Paris and Algeria; they held de Gaulle responsible for it since he was preaching respect for the classic and traditional rules of war that they thought inapplicable in Algeria.

This split continued to widen. While

French policy was turning its back on integration from the fall of 1958, the doctrines and psychology of the army seemed to be hardening. It was between 1958 and 1960 that the services of psychological action were most extended. At the same time, the reserve officers were, one might say, contaminated; the study of "revolutionary war" became the central theme of their work which was based, very officially, on this axiom: "Revolutionary war is one of the methods of Marxism-Leninism for seizing power...." De Gaulle did not attribute great importance to this evolution in the army. For him, military operations in Algeria ought to keep their limited, and thus classical, character. Their only goal was to destroy the organized forces of the FLN and to convince the enemy that it would be permitted no kind of success. Meanwhile, political, economic, and social action would turn the Algerians little by little away from the rebellion and would rally them to the "democratic" paths that France offered them. Nothing exasperated him more than the propensity of the military to busy themselves with everything and to behave, as he said, like children's nurses. The character of military activity seemed to him incompatible with the psychological or social tasks that excited a large part of the army, and any confusion of roles seemed to him bad....

After September 16, many officers judged that the moment had come for new political intervention. Many of them believed that the principle of self-determination was of itself disastrous. If the future referendum was to be absolutely free, would not the supporters of Algerian independence have complete liberty to express themselves and to campaign? Was this not legalizing in advance the propaganda and aims of the FLN?... [After a conference with de Gaulle in Paris on January 22, 1960, General Challe realized that] de Gaulle's words had a precise meaning: he would not change his policy and would even refuse on several matters—information, propaganda, repression—to give in to the pressure that was put upon him. From this time on Challe was disposed to favor any measure that could impress de Gaulle, for he was convinced that without a different policy everything he was doing in Algeria would prove itself useless. When Challe was informed that the demonstration of January 24 —forbidden in principle—would take place in spite of everything, he did not object, on condition that it remain within certain limits. But on the evening of January 24 a sudden burst of shooting caused the death of seventeen policemen and nine demonstrators. Challe could not ignore what de Gaulle expected of him; he immediately proclaimed a curfew.

De Gaulle, who had returned during that night from Colombey-les-deux-Eglises to Paris, at once issued a warning to the rioters, demanding that they "restore order" and warning them that he would do "his duty." From then on, he did not change his attitude. Impatient and wearied, he was convinced, at heart, that the European opposition was neither solid nor serious and that it would be foolish to make the slightest concession to it. It appeared evident to him that the passive complicity of several parachutist colonels had allowed the rioters to reinforce the barricades that had been fairly stripped during the night. In the Council of Ministers on the 25th, he was quite categorical: "The insurrection," he said, "must be put down." He openly challenged the representative character of the Algerian deputies and recognized that the army, as a whole, was hostile to his policy.... On the evening of the 29th, he put on his uniform to speak on television. The tone he used, his insistence in demanding discipline in the army, his condemnation of "the obliging indecisiveness of certain military elements," left no doubt of his intention to break the opposition of the barricades and of the colonels. Moreover, he once more excluded the possibility of treating the rebels "as the only valid representation." He added that "if one day the Moslems were to decide freely and formally that tomorrow's Algeria should be tightly united to France, nothing would cause more joy to the country and to de Gaulle than seeing them choose, between this or that solution, the one that would be the most French." To the army, which he said was "in the act of winning victory in Algeria," he promised, "When the time comes for moving to consultation, you will have to guarantee its complete and sincere freedom." Finally, he admitted that "the measures to be used to ensure that law remains strong could be of various kinds."

But at the end of several days, no uncertainty remained over the government's resolve to make use of the failure of the barricades. In the twenty-four hours preceding the surrender of Pierre Lagaillarde,[5] orders for an assault against the uprising's redoubt were still in force. It required a passionate intervention by several soldiers—especially of General de Beaufort—to postpone its execution to permit the surrender to to take place without bloodshed. Then Colonels Godard, Broizat, and Argoud were transferred to the mainland. Colonel Gardes was put on trial. The de-

[5] Leader of the Algerian students' union, which had set up barricades in Algiers.—Ed.

parture of Challe was virtually decided; it only took effect when he could occupy the post of commander of the Land Forces Central Europe of the Atlantic Alliance. General Crépin, who succeeded him, was reported to have no ties with the European community. The Offices of Psychological Action were abolished in all the general staffs. The Territorial Units, which served in practice as an armed force for the European community, were dissolved. *L' Echo d'Alger* was put under sequestration.

At this date, de Gaulle attained his highest degree of popularity in French opinion. The institutes of public opinion put at more than 65 percent the proportion of French people satisfied with his policy. He was convinced that he had broken the army's resistance, weakened permanently the activist organizations, proved the weakness of the European minority, and convinced the Moslem masses of the sincerity of his intentions. He hoped, now, that he had traveled the major part of the road that would lead to the Algerian settlement....

[On June 14, 1960] he publicly renewed his offers: "Once again, I turn ... to the leaders of the rebellion. I tell them that we are awaiting them here to find with them an honorable end to the struggles that are still dragging on, to settle the outcome of the armed conflict, and to determine the fate of those fighting. . . ." On June 25, after the FLN had agreed to send emissaries to organize the journey of Ferhat Abbas to Paris, conversations began at Melun. They broke off four days later. . . . The conversations at Melun had confirmed the FLN's determination not to engage in any purely military negotiation. In fact, the Algerian leaders, discussing the French offers, had no illusions; de Gaulle was not offering them political negotiation yet. However, they thought it preferable to establish proof of this by agreeing to send representatives to France. The credit de Gaulle had acquired in world opinion made it difficult for the FLN to give a systematic refusal. But its goal was to prove clearly that the French government had in view a cease-fire only. . . .

From July to November 1960, four months passed without any apparent change. However, it was then that de Gaulle took the decisions that were to result sixteen months later in the end of the war. The press, the parties, and the trade unions believed that they saw in them the decisive step toward a return of peace. Without any doubt, French opinion, profoundly disappointed by the failure of the talks, was expecting new proposals and was not resigning itself any longer to the continuance of the war. So de Gaulle felt it necessary to emphasize that the failure of Melun was the fault primarily of the FLN. Traveling through Normandy, he declared at Saint-Lô:

Those who, for reasons that are theirs and not ours, are more or less delaying the final outcome, to them, I say, without rancor, without hatred, for tomorrow everyone will be needed for that great Algerian work, I say to them that in delaying that moment they are wrong.

Then, at Rouen, he outlined several traits of the future Algeria, but in such a way that it appeared as a sovereign state:

It will be an Algerian Algeria, that is understood. But it will be necessary that all the communities, especially the French community, should have their place in its institutions, its government, its justice, and its Assemblies. . . .

De Gaulle was not unaware that he was preparing to give up everything that was properly "French" in Algeria: he was to be inevitably accused of having given up his first intentions—if not even his promises. He foresaw that terrible opposition was going to be expressed. He knew already that he was going to stake all his authority and all his prestige on taking away from France the sovereignty it exercised over a vast territory. In the fall of 1960 he resolved to do so.

First, there was the speech of November 4, in which he spoke for the first time of the Algerian republic "which will exist one day." Thus the goal was defined. . . .

[Negotiations with the FLN at Evian-les-Bains] opened on May 20, 1961. It quickly appeared that the Algerians intended to discuss the political and military conditions of self-determination only, whereas the French were trying to bring about an exchange of views on the future status of Algeria. This divergence of aim hid, in reality, a precise disagreement. By directing the discussion onto the self-determination referendum, the FLN had one aim: it wanted the area where the referendum would be held to be defined. In other words, it wanted to have the French accept immediately that the Sahara departments would be part of Algeria. While waiting for that decision, it had no interest in agreeing to the least concession on the status of the European minority. By contrast, the fate of that minority was of first importance to the French delegation. It was determined to concede nothing on the conditions of self-determination as long as it had not obtained the guarantee of the rights to be recognized to the Frenchmen of Algeria and the definition of the special ties between France and the future Algerian state. . . . De Gaulle decided that it was useless to continue so long as the FLN would not agree to seek a settlement of the future of Algeria; on June 13 he recalled the French delegation.

Actually, contacts were maintained. The French government believed that it was possible to resume the negotiations at once on two levels: the status of the European community and the Sahara. On this basis, conversations began again at Lugrin on July 20. But the Algerian negotiators—at least the majority among them—considered it dangerous to bind themselves on the first point as long as they were in no way assured that the French would cede definitively on the second. On July 28 they broke off the discussions. . . .

Before the end of September, the French representatives confirmed to the FLN leaders the decision taken by de Gaulle: by whatever method, the Sahara would be Algerian. At once, negotiations were resumed. Both sides even considered that they would be completed by the end of the year. It was understood that the FLN would participate in the provisional executive that would preside over the self-determination of Algeria. Between the two sides, a "cooperation" agreement would

be concluded that would be immediately applicable after its ratification by the Algerians, on the same day as the self-determination vote. There one saw the constant preoccupations of the French government: status of the European minority, provisional maintenance of the military bases, protection of property and investments, guarantee of the established interests in the Sahara. Doubtless, the agreements would have been concluded much more quickly if the internal difficulties of the FLN— both practical and political—had not slowed down the rhythm of the negotiations. Until their conclusion on March 18 [1962], de Gaulle continued in his distrust of the ability and clear-sightedness of the leaders of the FLN. But he was determined to allow the negotiations to continue to their completion. He pressed his representatives to end them as quickly as possible. He sharply dismissed the idea of an autonomous State, set up by the European community on a portion of Algerian territory, as suggested by Jean Sarradet, one of the heads of the OAS. Basically, de Gaulle considered that the Algerian affair was virtually settled from October on. For him, the last page in the history of decolonization had been turned.

With the acceptance of the Evian Agreements in both France and Algeria by the referendum of July 1962, it became possible to make a preliminary judgment on the manner in which de Gaulle had finally brought about an end to the Algerian problem and on the cost to France of its achievement. DOROTHY PICKLES (1903–   ), who directed the French section of the BBC during World War II, and has written several books on the Fourth and Fifth Republics, points out, in *Algeria and France: From Colonialism to Cooperation* (1963), that whereas there was much justified criticism of timing and "devious" methods, no other solution was possible, and only de Gaulle could have achieved it. The real price of Gaullist policy, she believes, lay in political problems, outside the field of Algerian policy, which arose from de Gaulle's being given a free hand in French government in return for dealing with the Algerian problem.*

General de Gaulle and Algeria: Success or Failure?

If, as it appears, it is France's position in Western Europe and in NATO, and her status in the world, that are and always have been General de Gaulle's predominating preoccupations, then the extent to which his Algerian policy can be regarded as a success or a failure must really be judged by the answers to a number of questions. First, if the Algerian problem could be regarded as settled, as far as France was concerned, by the referendum of July [1962], were the conditions in which the war was ended, and the terms of the agreement, a vindication of his Algerian policy or not? Had there been errors of method

¹ Secret Army Organization, terrorist group organized by European settlers in Algeria to prevent the grant of independence.—Ed.

or timing? Was the OAS¹ terror campaign in Algeria, which followed the cease-fire, in part a result of France's own policies? Had self-determination come too late, and in such conditions that the wholesale repatriation of the European community could no longer be prevented, thus making Algerian independence in association with France impossible to achieve in practice? Further, even if there had been serious mistakes, did it necessarily follow that any better solution of the Algerian problem could have been reached, in any circumstances, by either General de Gaulle or anyone else? Finally, whatever the degree of success or failure of his Algerian policy, what has been, or is likely to be, the cost of it to France in other fields?

* From Dorothy Pickles, *Algeria and France: From Colonialism to Cooperation* (London: Methuen, 1963; New York: Praeger, 1963), pp. 138–143, 146–152, 154–155, 157–160. Reprinted by permission of Methuen and Co. Ltd., and Frederick A. Praeger, Inc. Footnotes omitted.

Time's Revenges

There were two main criticisms of the President's Algerian policy. The first was essentially a criticism of timing. Few had expected, in 1958, that it would take four years to reach a settlement, and that, when it was reached, the authority of the French state, as well as the future of the new Algerian Republic, would be threatened by the activities of the OAS. Could the result have been achieved earlier, before the OAS had become strong enough to present the danger that it constituted in 1962? A year went by between the breakdown of the Melun negotiations and the breakdown of the talks at Evian and Lugrin, and a further six or seven months went by before the official resumption of talks.[2] Was the delay caused by FLN intransigence? If so, what made the FLN leaders eventually accept terms which most French people considered to be eminently reasonable, but which the FLN leaders themselves criticized later as having included too many concessions to French demands? Or was the delay caused by the rigidity of the French, by their unwillingness to make concessions except grudgingly and too late? For instance, if France had been prepared to concede at Melun what was finally conceded fourteen months later by General de Gaulle in a press conference and a broadcast, would it have been possible to avoid the insurrection of April 1961? or alternatively, if the concession had been made a year later, could agreement perhaps have been reached at Evian?

Until more information is available on the reasons for the breakdown of the

1960 and 1961 talks, it is possible only to speculate on the extent to which General de Gaulle, or his representatives, or the FLN, mishandled these abortive conversations. In neither case did it appear that the talks ever progressed beyond the stage of trying to work out an agenda, and the successful final talks were preceded by months of private negotiations. All this is consistent with the thesis that, at that stage, both sides were intransigent, and that the stimulus to reach an early agreement came more from FLN fears of the OAS than from the President's decision in the autumn of 1961 to play the "now or never" card, though this may have helped. The readiness of the Algerian Provisional Government, in spite of all the OAS violence and provocation in the weeks following the cease-fire, to seek an agreement that might halt the exodus of the European population does at least indicate that the FLN might well have been alarmed at the President's threat of "disengagement," a threat which, if carried out, would have produced a similar exodus. It may be significant that the President had indicated a time limit, namely, the end of the year or thereabouts, and that the FLN had agreed sufficiently with the French spokesmen to be able to open official talks by the beginning of February [1962]. The whole sequence of events seems to indicate that neither side was really in a hurry until the OAS threat became acute in France, and so also a threat to Algeria. For if France were to succumb to disorder, or to a military coup, that would have put an end to Algerian independence in association with France.

If this was in reality what happened, then final success was due less to General de Gaulle than to the chief enemies of his policy, and the very strength of these enemies was an indication of the failure

[2] Peace talks with the FLN began at Melun, near Paris, on June 25, 1960, but were broken off after four days. New negotiations at Evian on the Swiss border lasted from May 20 to June 13, 1961. A third attempt at Lugrin in Switzerland lasted only from July 20–28, 1961.—Ed.

of one of his main objectives, which was to settle the Algerian problem without destroying the unity of the army or causing civil war. He had gone to great lengths in order to avoid advertising the extent of division and disloyalty in the army. The purges of 1959 were so discreet as to be only partially effective, and the refusal to make any martyrs helped to make future insurrections possible. In the second of these,[3] nearly three years after General de Gaulle's return to power, army units and high army officers were directly participating in a rebellion against the state, and, in the ensuing OAS campaign in Algeria, French soldiers eventually had to fire on other Frenchmen.

General de Gaulle may be said, then, to have failed, in that he had to pay a price for the achievement of a cease-fire that he had not intended to pay. . . .

Here again, one can only speculate. If reports at the time were accurate, it did seem that the Melun talks broke down on questions of status before any agenda could even be discussed, and that neither side was really prepared to make any real concessions. A year later [1961], the main stumbling block appeared to be the difference on the question of sovereignty over the Sahara, but comment on the Bizerte crisis made it quite clear that French opinion was expecting a struggle over the French right to remain in Mers-el-Kebir.[4] There were certainly criticisms of the belatedness of French concessions. The *de facto* recognition of the FLN leaders as authentic representatives of a future government was refused at Melun, and accorded a year later at Evian. French sovereignty (or rather some kind of international sovereignty) over the Sahara was affirmed at Evian in 1961 and Algerian sovereignty conceded a month or so later. But there is no evidence that, if the concessions had been made earlier, agreement on a cease-fire would have been any easier or any speedier. The most that can be said is that the manner in which concessions were withheld was often one that was bound to exasperate easily offended nationalists. On the other hand, to judge by some remarks of M. Joxe,[5] the French delegation had to put up with a good deal of evasion and demagogy from FLN spokesmen.

The accusation of mistiming must, therefore, for the time being and until the full facts are known, be considered as unproven. There is nothing to suggest that, once OAS resistance had collapsed, General de Gaulle had any reason to be dissatisfied with the terms of the agreements, or that he could have achieved them any sooner than he did. Even if the FLN was less intransigent than has generally been supposed, the facts of army unreliability and the active hostility to his policy in some circles in France would have compelled him to move cautiously. It has sometimes been suggested that he ought to have moved quickly after the January referendum of 1961, which really gave him a blank check to prepare for Algerian self-determination. But three months after the bill became law, he had to face the April insurrection, followed by yet another

[3] The army revolt of April 22–26, 1961, led by Generals Salan, Jouhaud, Challe and Zeller.—Ed.

[4] The French sought to retain control over the Sahara because of the recent development of vast oil deposits there. Bizerte, the French naval base in Tunisia, which was claimed by the Tunisian government, was attacked in 1961 by a Tunisian mob and defended with much bloodshed by the French forces. In negotiating with the FLN, the French demanded the right to remain in Mers-el-Kebir, a naval and air base in Algeria.—Ed.

[5] Minister of State for Algerian Affairs and principal French negotiator of the Evian agreements.—Ed.

(the third) series of army and civil-service purges. General de Gaulle had to do the job with the tools that he had, and they were not always either reliable or effective.

Wherever responsibility lay, however, the fact that it took nearly four years to achieve a cease-fire was certainly regarded as constituting a failure on the part of General de Gaulle by those who had been expecting him to accomplish miracles. Criticisms of his timing were, in reality, part of much wider criticisms of his methods in general in dealing with the Algerian problem. The extent of disaffection in the army was held by some to be attributable, at least in part, to the President's methods. He had, perhaps, assumed too easily that his personality and his authority would be enough to rally the support of dissident army officers to the Republic and to make the army a reliable executant of his policy. As one commentator remarked, his problem was in reality less simple than Napoleon's had been in persuading the Chouan rebels to stop fighting. But, for his critics, the President's mistakes went far deeper than mere errors of judgment. In their view, his methods had actually helped to increase disunity and disloyalty in the army, thus adding in the short run to the difficulties presented by the Algerian problem, and threatening in the long run to add to France's difficulties in the aftermath of the Algerian war.

The Price of Ambiguity

There is no doubt that many Frenchmen who believed in General de Gaulle's policy and welcomed the terms of the cease-fire felt nevertheless that France would have to pay a high price for what were often described as his "devious" methods. Many supporters of *Algérie*

française, and especially many army officers, had trusted him to keep Algeria French. For months they had not known exactly where he stood, and the broadcast of September 1959, in which General de Gaulle announced his policy of self-determination for Algeria, not only came as a terrible shock, but was resented as a betrayal. This sense of betrayal has already been mentioned in connection with the trials of officers involved in the April insurrection. It was used later at the trials of ex-Generals Jouhaud and Salan, both by the defense and by the accused themselves, to excuse the activities of the OAS. . . .

It was partly this consciousness that the European population had legitimate grounds for feeling betrayed that led many French people to feel that, as an Algerian, General Jouhaud had an authentic claim to the verdict of extenuating circumstances which they denied to General Salan. The court that tried both and condemned General Jouhaud to death clearly felt (though only by a majority of one) that General Salan had had reason to feel that he had been deceived.

The exponent of a political philosophy based on personal leadership is in a peculiarly vulnerable position. He cannot be absolved from all responsibility if those who accept his leadership assume that he means what they believe him to have said. To fool the people is easier than some democrats have thought. It is none the less a dangerous adventure, and even more so when, on the one hand, the people are indulging in the kind of wishful thinking that makes it all the easier to fool them—as was the case with Algerian supporters of *Algérie française*—and when, on the other hand, the chief casualty of the operation is likely to be faith in the leader. This means that the cost of the Algerian operation as General de Gaulle conducted it was likely to include opposition, not only to him, but also to the institutions and policies of the Fifth Republic associated with his conception of leadership.

The Art of the Possible

Leaving out of account these criticisms of timing and of methods, what can be said about the Algerian policy itself? Here we are immediately in the realm of speculation, for it still has to be proved that the Evian agreements will turn out to be a workable basis for future Franco-Algerian cooperation, and, even if they do not, that any more satisfactory solution of the problem was ever possible in the circumstances in which General de Gaulle found himself.

What must not be forgotten is that, in reality, there was never a choice between some ideal solution and a varying number of more or less satisfactory compromises. Military victory was either unattainable in any circumstances or conceivable only at the cost of a full-scale war of conquest, which was never seriously contemplated by anyone but a handful of the more unrealistic army officers. To those who sincerely believed in a policy of integration, such a victory would, in any case, have been self-defeating. Indeed, one of the main weaknesses of the "tough" military activist position was precisely the fundamental contradiction inherent in the assumption that the Moslems were enemies who had to be conquered in order to allow them to satisfy their basic wish to remain French! The contradiction could be evaded for a time by the pretense that the rebels were a minority of criminals supported by sinister interests outside France and opposed to France. This was never very plausible and, from 1960 onward, was

demonstrably a fantasy. Acceptance of defeat, and the withdrawal of the army from an Algeria left to its own resources, was not contemplated by any section of opinion at all, and would in any case not have been accepted by the army. There remained, therefore, only the possibility of some compromise settlement, and all those contemplated were, for a number of reasons, either unattainable or undesirable or both. All of them were opposed by some sections of opinion in France.

They can, in effect, be reduced to four. It was possible for General de Gaulle, in theory at least, merely to try to go on stalling indefinitely, as the Fourth Republic had done. In this case, the Fifth Republic would rapidly have gone the same way as the Fourth and for the same reasons. The difference would have been that the military *coup d'état* would really have been tried, and might possibly have succeeded, instead of stopping short at a landing in Corsica. One of the main aims of General de Gaulle and of those who voted for him as head of the French Government was, in the first place, to prevent this. After four Prime Ministers whose well-meant efforts had brought France to the verge of civil war, and a fifth who had handed over military and civil powers to the leader of an insurrection, they wanted a government that could be expected to gain the loyalty of the soldiers as well as of the civilians.

Some opponents of General de Gaulle seemed prepared to try to call the bluff of the 1958 insurgents. M. Mendès-France, M. Mitterand, the small left-wing splinter group of the Socialist Party, some Radicals, and possibly the Communists seemed to be suggesting in 1958 that the Fourth Republic was at heart sounder than it seemed, and that the right course was to take the risk of civil war in France as well as in Algeria, in defense of the Republic and of republican institutions. This was never explicitly stated, nor was it evident at any point that any French Government had been able even to begin to formulate any coherent policy. All the evidence available at the time and since points to the conclusion that no such attempt could have been made and that, even if it could, the result would have been the same as in the previous hypothesis. The efforts made by the Communists, or by non-Communist trade unions, to bring out demonstrators met with a solid block of apathetic resistance. Families streamed away for the Whitsun holiday, not to the barricades. The single large left-wing demonstration (that of May 28) took place when the Fourth Republic was already virtually dead and, impressive though it was, could have contributed nothing concrete toward the defense of the Republic against armed paratroops. No outsider who has talked to the political leaders or journalists who lived through the events of May 13–31 in Paris, or in any large French city, is under any illusions on this. There was no will to fight and, even if the will had been there, there was no possibility. The conscript army was mainly in Algeria, and what forces there were in France included paratroops or ex-paratroops in sympathy with the insurrection. What the majority of the non-Communist Left were afraid of was anarchy in France and in Algeria, leading to a military dictatorship. M. Mollet supported General de Gaulle's return to power precisely because the danger was not that of civil war, but of surrender without fighting. Without General de Gaulle, he thought, "there would have been, not a civil war, but a 'Spanish war' without a republican army. We should have had a military dictatorship for twenty or thirty years." M. Mendès-France, on the other hand, opposed General de Gaulle's return to power in the circumstances of May 1958, because he thought this would lead to military dictatorship. "The pressure to which General de Gaulle will be subjected," he said, "from some of his strongest and most recent supporters . . . will speedily become formidable. Will de Gaulle be prepared to resist it? I hope so. Will he be able to? . . . With every day that passes, the increased demands of those who are already crying victory will make it more difficult." M. Mendès-France turned out to be wrong. Whatever happens in the future, at least France remained a Republic for four and a half years, and for that General de Gaulle could take the major share of the credit.

The third possibility was to aim at an agreement with the more moderate nationalists, the hoped-for "third force." This, as has been seen, proved to be an illusion. There remained, therefore, only the possibility of an agreement with the rebels themselves, on the best terms obtainable. In this case, whether or not General de Gaulle ever actually said that the choice was "at best, Houphouet-Boigny, at worst Sékou Touré,"[6] the alternatives represented by these two names—independence in association with France or secession—were the only remaining ones.

In the circumstances, therefore, M. Reynaud's verdict, that "the war did not end in favorable conditions, but in the only conditions that were possible,"

[6] Houphouet-Boigny, later President of the Ivory Coast, supported de Gaulle's plans in 1960 for giving autonomy within a French Community to France's black African territories; Sékou Touré, a Marxist, persuaded Guinea to chose complete independence.—Ed.

must be regarded as a vindication of General de Gaulle's policy. And all the evidence indicates that that is how the nation regarded it. The agreements were accepted by a large majority of the population in the April referendum (over 90 per cent of the voters and almost 65 per cent of the electorate), and only the Poujadists and a couple of small splinter groups still supporting a French Algeria advised their members to vote "No." In only one *département* (Corsica) was the number of affirmative votes less than 50 per cent of the electorate. Even the Communists advised their supporters to vote "Yes," explaining that this meant a vote for peace, but not for the man who had brought peace.

How and why did General de Gaulle succeed where previous governments had failed? To some extent, circumstances helped him as they had not helped his predecessors. There was growing war-weariness, fear of the OAS and of the moral deterioration that had come with prolonged terrorism. But his main assets were a combination of personal qualities and defects, together with what the French public and the political parties knew of his past and believed him likely to do in the future. To begin with, he had the advantage of not having been in any way associated with France's post-war Algerian policy, and so had no accumulation of Moslem distrust to contend with. On the contrary, what the Moslems knew of him inspired confidence. As head of the Provisional Government in Algiers in 1943–1944, he had restored French citizenship to Algerian Jews and extended the Moslem franchise. As head of the Government in 1958, he had taken the initiative of allowing all the French Overseas Territories to opt for immediate independence, and as head of the state had enabled twelve of them to accede to full independence within two years. They had, therefore, good reason to assume that his policy toward Algeria might be no less liberal.

Nor did General de Gaulle suffer from the discredit attached to politics and politicians in postwar France. As a republican, his record was impeccable. He had led the wartime resistance movement, but he had refused to use his popularity to make himself a dictator. On the contrary, he had resigned from the Premiership in 1946. He had subsequently led an opposition movement, and consistently criticized governments and politicians from 1947 to 1955, but it had been a movement aiming at power through constitutional means, and his own return to power in 1958 had been by means of a regular vote in the National Assembly. His detachment from parties was regarded by many people as an asset, and his methods of personal rule—the tours, broadcasts, press conferences—maintained his popularity with the public, which was asked merely to approve his policy. He remained, therefore, to a politically apathetic public, a national father-figure.

To political parties in the National Assembly, General de Gaulle offered an escape from a situation that governments had already ceased to be able to cope with, even before the danger of a military *coup d'état* became imminent. Whatever was eventually done about Algeria would unavoidably be unpopular—or so it seemed in 1958, and right up to the referendum of 1961. General de Gaulle had no electors to placate, and, as a soldier, he would be able to deal with the army, or so it was thought —wrongly, as it turned out.

General de Gaulle, who is at times an astute tactician, was thus able to profit from popular support, from political indispensability, and from his remoteness from the parliamentary "game of politics," in order to play his own game. His establishment of *de facto* personal rule enabled him to have what no government had had since the rebellion broke out, namely, a policy for Algeria. And the strength of his personality enabled him to exploit situations to his advantage. In 1958, M. Pflimlin, at the head of a newly formed government so divided that several of its members were threatening to resign when it was only a week old, had been able only to hand over responsibility to General Salan when the insurrection broke out in Algeria. When the two insurrections broke out during General de Gaulle's Presidency, he was demonstrably in charge.

His real authority in a crisis stems partly from his superb self-confidence, from his belief in his mission and in his capacity to act as France's guide. How it appears at its best has been well described in the following passage relating to the insurrection of April 1961:

He is at his best in the storm. He seems almost to be enjoying it, and it is a fact that it increases tenfold his capacities of maneuver and command. To those around him, he appears unruffled. To ministers whose reactions he wants to test, he seems to be under no illusions. They think that they are sounding *him*. In reality, it is he who is weighing *them*.

He is in no hurry to show his hand, or to throw the weight of his own words into the scales. He waits until the balance is already beginning to tilt to his advantage. For nothing is worse than orders without effect or words that produce no echo.

The Cost of Gaullist Policy

For the politicians of the Fourth Republic, General de Gaulle's leadership and the new institutions were essentially part of a package deal. Since he was indispensable in the matter of Algeria, he was in a position to insist on the acceptance of what is generally (not altogether accurately) thought of as *his* Constitution and of what were certainly *his* policies. But Presidential rule was thought of by all except the Gaullists as an interlude. The Presidential monologue was justified only by the gravity of the situation.

Both sides saw the political climate as justifying their own views. And since their concepts of how the political machine ought to function were totally antithetic, they naturally arrived at antithetic conclusions. For the President, the real France was the public, and particularly the crowd, the ordinary citizens who lined the streets on his provincial tours. When he continued, as he did, to pay tribute to the efficacy of the new system, to the stability that France owed to the new institutions, and to contrast the weaknesses and vacillations of the past with the present "serenity" and sureness of purpose of a united nation, he was thinking of this relation between President and people. And in this context, his idyllic picture was not totally unrealistic. The general public was "serene" enough, though whether owing to political apathy or to enthusiasm for his leadership, as he liked to assume, was a matter of opinion. He treated opposition to his policies as an unfortunate hangover from the bad old days. Politicians who attacked them were "snarlers, grumblers, and grousers," whose antics no longer really counted. It was natural, therefore, that the ending of the Algerian problem should be seen by the President as an opportunity to take further steps along this new road, which suited France—his "real France"—so well.

For the leaders of the political parties, however, this picture bore no relation to the facts. For them, the political opinions that counted were those of the elected representatives in the Assembly and the Senate. These were the accredited spokesmen for France—*le pays légal.* And they saw government in normal circumstances, neither in terms of Presidential leadership, technocratic ministers, and a subservient Parliament, nor in terms of a Presidential image, projected by tours and broadcasts, and Presidential popularity bolstered by referendums. They saw it in terms of general elections and parliamentary government by a responsible Prime Minister. With the end of the "interlude" occasioned by the Algerian problem in sight, this was what they wanted to go back to. The "snarlers and grousers" were looking forward to the end of the Fifth Republic, and less violent objectors to a gradual return to more normal political habits.

There were three principal sources of conflict between President and parties. There was first, of course, the Constitution itself, which the more moderate wanted to amend, and the others to get rid of. Interpretation of some of its provisions had led to direct clashes between President and Parliament, but the main objection of the majority to it lay not in the provisions themselves, but in the way they had been used by the President as an instrument of personal rule. They resented, in the second place, the President's attitude to Parliament, as well as his conception of its role in the state. He had ignored it where he could, chosen his second Prime Minister from outside both parties and Parliament, and intervened directly in fields that they thought ought to be the responsibility of ministers, subject to the

approval of Parliament. And thirdly, a majority of deputies were increasingly opposed to the President's attempts to reverse the course of France's European and NATO policies. . . .

The de Gaulle Problem

In the months following the Algerian settlement, it certainly looked as if one of the first consequences of the settlement of the Algerian problem would be its replacement by the de Gaulle problem. For it seemed to many politicians that the President, his attitudes and his methods, and not Algeria, now "blocked all roads." To non-Gaullists, it seemed obvious that what had been achieved in Algeria owed everything to the man and nothing to the institutions. It was possible that the President's use of some of the new instruments of Presidential power—the threat of dissolution, for instance—had deterred deputies from succumbing to the temptation to translate their resentment into votes. But it was not very probable, for he had even more effective weapons at his command which had nothing to do with the Constitution. The most effective deterrent had always been the fear of deputies, including those in opposition to him, that he would resign before an Algerian settlement had been reached. Some of the new constitutional rules, together with M. Debré's manipulation of the governmental instruments for controlling the Assembly, had no doubt spared the Prime Minister many wearisome hours of Assembly debate, and a great many votes of confidence. The result, however, would have been the same in any case. But once Algerian independence was a fact, whether the President really needed either the powers given specifically to him in the Constitution or those that he took himself, sometimes with dubious constitutional authority, was no longer important. What mattered then was whether these powers were to be used in any other circumstances than those governed by the Algerian situation, or by anyone other than President de Gaulle.

In his broadcast in June 1962, General de Gaulle referred only in characteristically vague and ambiguous terms to the need to look "beyond men who come and go" and to ensure the "strength, order, and continuity of the Republic." Press comments promptly spoke of him as "taking the road to Bonapartism," as "seeking to challenge and overcome the forces of democracy," as "expressing satisfaction with himself and contempt for other men," as having "a conception of the Republic which failed to recognize the essential role of Parliament in a democracy."

At the opening of the autumn Parliamentary session, there came the first head-on clash between the President and the non-Gaullist parties. On September 20, General de Gaulle had announced his intention to hold yet another referendum, this time to secure approval for a constitutional revision providing for the election of future Presidents by universal suffrage. Virtually all parties except the Gaullists opposed either the proposal itself, the President's method of introducing it, or both. In the view of most jurists, as well as most politicians, constitutional revision by referendum only was unconstitutional. Party leaders resented, too, what they regarded as yet another attempt by the President to belittle the role of Parliament, and one that amounted to a declaration of war against the Parliamentary system itself. A motion of censure was, therefore, tabled, and, in the early hours of October 5, the Government was defeated.

The President's reply to what was, in reality, an attack on him was to dissolve the National Assembly.

The referendum held on October 28 was a victory for the President, in that his proposal was accepted by the majority of the voters. It was a defeat in that it did not provide him with the spectacular vote of confidence that he had asked for. Together, no's and abstentions accounted for more than 50 per cent of the electorate. The President had threatened to resign if he did not receive a substantial majority in the referendum. It was generally anticipated that the elections would prove less favorable to him than the referendum. The prediction frequently made by critics of the regime, that Gaullism would not outlive the emergency created by the Algerian war seemed, therefore, likely to be fulfilled, unless General de Gaulle was prepared for a prolonged struggle with Parliament, with all the risks of political instability that that would entail.

In May 1958, in a letter to ex-President Auriol, General de Gaulle had envisaged the possibility that "an incomprehensible factionalism," as he put it, might prevent him from "once again saving the Republic." If that happened, he said, "There will be nothing left for me but to spend the rest of my days with my grief."

History will certainly record that he did, indeed, save the Republic twice. On both these occasions, the majority of the Parliamentary leaders were on his side. This had ceased to be true even before the clash over the constitutional amendment. As one commentator wrote in June:

His mission is coming to an end. Apart from the fact that it was entrusted to him by the country, there were no rival candidates for the job, least of all among the politicians.

The situation is different now. The politicians whom he has ousted feel themselves to be better qualified than he is to rebuild France, defend the Republic, and create Europe.

In the elections at the end of 1962, however, the public did not support the politicians. Nevertheless, the Gaullist victory could not hide the fact that, in 1962, France was even more divided than she had been in 1958. The Army's relation to the state, the future of the regime, the role of political parties— all these problems were still unresolved, as were those of France's defense and European policies. In all these fields, the President was himself an additional cause of disunity, and there was, as yet, no certainty that the political parties would even be able to agree, either on a Presidential candidate or on the role that they wanted the next President to play.

During his years in the political wilderness, General de Gaulle is said to have remarked that he had succeeded only in time of war and that, with the coming

of peace, his compatriots had "ceased to understand." At the end of 1962, they seemed to have ceased to care. Under the Presidency of General de Gaulle, the Fifth Republic had become a regime of *de facto* personal rule in a political vacuum. This atmosphere of public apathy, no less than the President's positive antipathy to political parties, helped to account for the continued impotence of opposition parties and perhaps, to some extent, for the failure of the majority party, the Gaullist UNR, to develop any of the characteristics of a genuine political party. It also hindered the process of elimination from the body politic of the specific political poisons introduced into it by the Algerian problem itself. It seems likely, therefore, that, whenever and however General de Gaulle's Presidency ends, his political methods outside the field of his Algerian policy will leave France with a host of political problems that she may well be psychologically and politically ill-equipped to solve.

The action of de Gaulle that most outraged his five partners in the Common Market, and indeed all supporters of European unification, was his veto of British membership, pronounced at his press conference on January 14, 1963. The fury of those who had worked for a generation to bring about the union of all free Europe is expressed in this extract by ERNST FRIEDLAENDER (1895–   ), former president of Europa-Union Deutschland, West Germany's principal federalist organization, and KATHARINA FOCKE (1922–   ), business manager of Bildungswerk Europäische Politik, which coordinates the educational work of several German federalist groups. They see de Gaulle's nationalism as a great, but probably ephemeral, challenge to the course Europe ought to follow in the twentieth century—supranationalism.*

One Man Against Europe

In the age of supranationalism de Gaulle towers like an archaic figure from the nineteenth, and at times from the seventeenth, century. The sovereign nation state is for him the last and the highest, and indeed the only, reality in the political world of Europe. But most important of all for him is the Great Power position, the World Power position, of the nation state of France. This France, beside the United States and Great Britain, must be the third leading power of the West. And most of all, at the head of Europe, he wants to see something like a third force in world affairs beside the United States and the Soviet Union. This "at the head of Europe" is an integral part of

de Gaulle's political conception, since, however much he may value France, he knows very well that it cannot reach its sky-high goals alone. De Gaulle needs Europe, but he needs it, as it were, as a means to a national, French purpose. Hence, nothing further can be sacrificed of French national sovereignty. Hence, a form must be found in which France can appear as the spokesman of Europe to the outside world, with all the additional weight that this role brings. This Europe of the states does not include England, since in a Europe with England there would be no leadership role for France, or any appreciable increase in French power.

Germany, however, will as surely be

* From Ernst Friedlaender and Katharina Focke, *Europa über den Nationen* (Cologne: Bildungswerk Europäische Politik, 1963), pp. 85–88. Translated by editor.

included as England will be excluded. To make this possible, and for France to be the leader and spokesman of Europe, Germany will be given a special role in Europe's internal affairs. In internal affairs, Germany will stand beside France as its closest friend and partner. Internally, France and Germany share leadership so that in external matters France can lead as far as possible alone. So we see: the membership of this Europe is the same as that of the Europe of the Six who got together in the Coal and Steel Community, the Common Market, and Euratom. It is the spirit of that supranational Europe of which nothing remains. All the ideas have been twisted. De Gaulle once represented himself, in one of his boldest statements, as the completer of the work of Robert Schuman. In reality, he constitutes the extreme pole to everything that Schuman desired and did. Everything fits together: the call for a three-power directorate in NATO, the independent atomic power as a *force de frappe,* the attempt, by land, sea, and air, to remove the greatest possible forces from NATO, the denial of American requests, the sharp exclusion of England [from the Common Market], the courting of the "great nation" of Germany. Here is once again great power politics carried out with all the weapons of the past. The balance of power is again rampant, and hegemony, alliance under the banner of one leading country, the sovereign state devoted only to its own interests, and the state which is identified with a single man for whom there is no successor.

The grandiose character of this opposition of the past to the future can scarcely be denied. There have also been grandiose mistakes in world history; this is not the first. Only unfortu-

nately it is true that the mistake, the anachronism, in politics can have as much reality as the right and the timely action. De Gaulle's Fifth Republic is undeniably a reality. It may be considered ephemeral, since it can scarcely survive him. But so long as de Gaulle is at its head, one must reckon with it and live with it.

Moreover, supporters of a supranational Europe cannot ignore this fact. To live with de Gaulle could mean for the supranational to live in spite of de Gaulle, and not to perish in spite of de Gaulle. But in order to clarify this, it must be asked what de Gaulle is now really opposing to the supranational in internal European matters. A long time ago de Gaulle and the Gaullist party plunged into European events, bitterly opposing both the Coal and Steel Community and the European Defense Community. Already at that time de Gaulle had raised as a counter-idea in the debate the concept of a European "confederation," without, however, defining in detail what was to be understood by it. At de Gaulle's press conference in February 1953, he spoke of a ruling council of heads of government and of a referendum of the European peoples to approve the confederation. At that early stage de Gaulle, it seems, was thinking not of a Europe of the Six but of the whole of free Europe, including England.

De Gaulle is well known for holding on to his basic ideas with extraordinary tenacity. Thus, as President of France, he has never renounced his conception of Europe but has simply made it clearly applicable only to the Europe of the Six. Like a red flag, through many declarations of de Gaulle in press conference and television speeches as well as in governmental conferences, the slogan is raised: organized political co-operation of the six governments, refusal of the supranational idea, later perhaps a "confederation." Details like the creation of a political secretariat in Paris or the popular referendum in the six states he has changed or dropped completely. In important matters he has remained true to himself. . . .

The signing of the Franco-German Treaty of Cooperation was on the program for January 1963. In the same month the fifteen-month-old negotiations between the six EEC states and Britain on Britain's application for membership in EEC were to be resumed. These talks had been extremely difficult in detailed matters, but as a result of the readiness of both sides to make concessions, a successful outcome that would not impair the substance of the treaty was near. Basically, Britain needed to be guaranteed transitional concessions to carry out the ending of Commonwealth preference and to find a solution to the problem of agrarian policy. It seemed as though the achievement of a wider Europe could soon be achieved without sacrificing any part of the depth of European unification already gained. An advance toward deeper supranationalism was blocked by the veto of France. But the conviction remained that the Fifth Republic had, although unwillingly, reconciled itself to the widening of EEC.

All these hopes were disappointed. At his press conference of January 14, 1963, de Gaulle showed his true self as never before. In contradiction of the obvious facts, he described the negotiations with Britain as having no chance of success. This press conference was nothing less than de Gaulle's veto on Britain's membership in EEC. It was clear beyond doubt that the reason for the veto was not to be found in the details of the negotiations and especially not in the economic sphere. De Gaulle closed the door on Britain because he can only maintain the French claim to leadership in the absence of Britain. Only without Britain and against the United States can he pursue his policy of a third force in world politics. The anti-Atlantic aim is as clear here as the anti-British. England in EEC, for him, would be the Trojan Horse of the United States in Europe. The European Communities, conceived as a beginning, and hence kept open to all states of free Europe, by the will of de Gaulle and within the framework of France's Great Power policy must remain "little Europe" and must not be widened.

With this press conference it was made clear that the negotiations on Britain's entry into EEC must fail. New members, according to the treaty, can be admitted only by the unanimous vote of the original members. Thus, there was no possibility of setting aside de Gaulle's veto. After a short delay, the negotiations broke down fourteen days after the press conference. All efforts of the five partners who supported Britain's entry were useless.

But between the next-to-last and last conference of the foreign ministers of the EEC states, the Franco-German Treaty of Friendship was ceremoniously signed. That was an extremely unfortunate coincidence, which once again gave rise to misgivings. De Gaulle had planned this as well. He had imposed his veto shortly before such an action would have come within the consultation requirement of the new treaty and also before the ratification could have failed as a result of the spirit of his veto. The veto came, moreover, immediately before further negotiations on Britain's acceptance into EEC. It came not because the negotiations were going too badly but rather because they were going too well. De Gaulle had hoped for a long time that the negotiations might fail without his having to play his last card. Since these expectations were not fulfilled, he showed without ambiguity or reticence that he stood alone against Europe.

January 1963 has been compared with August 1954.[1] It is true that both oc-

[1] On August 30, 1954, the French National Assembly rejected the European Defense Community Treaty by which an integrated European army was to be created.—Ed.

casions were black days for Europe, but the comparison is not quite sound. The European Defense Community was wrecked on the opposition of the majority of the elected representatives of France. Britain's membership in EEC was wrecked on the opposition of a single man, General de Gaulle.

One man against Europe—it is a sufficient paradox that such a thing is still possible in the democratic age in the West. But at the same time there is also hope in this fact. For what will be stronger in the long run: the stubborn will of one man whose Fifth Republic will not outlive him or the historic forces and necessities of our century?

At no time does de Gaulle give the appearance of a prophet unraveling the future for the benefit of his short-sighted contemporaries more than in his foreign policy pronouncements. Yet it is in this sphere above all that he has been attacked for being out-of-date. ALFRED GROSSER (1925–   ), research director of the National Foundation of Political Sciences in Paris and author of *The Foreign Policy of the Fifth Republic,* writing in *International Affairs* for a British audience three months after de Gaulle's veto on British membership in the Common Market, attempts to evaluate de Gaulle's foreign policy as a whole. He points out that many of de Gaulle's aims are forward-looking, but that the veto on British membership was a mistake, in that it did not achieve de Gaulle's own purpose.*

► Positive Aspects of Foreign Policy

Hated or admired, sometimes admired then hated, often hated and admired simultaneously, General de Gaulle stands, at the beginning of 1963, at the front of the Western political stage. Only a few months ago leaders and journalists across the Channel, the Rhine and the Atlantic were extravagantly praising the great statesman who had known how to give independence to Algeria. Today there is unbridled rage against the arrogant monster who is destroying Europe. Yet this is one and the same man. In France the electors have largely followed his wholehearted admirers, but the former political class feel their unreserved condemnation of him

to have been confirmed by the European crisis. Intransigence and intolerance reign. One is anti-Gaullist to the extent that one criticises, Gaullist to the extent that one approves.

It would be a good thing if in Paris, no less than in Washington and London, it were possible to call an emotional truce so that the man and his policies could be analysed calmly and rationally. An understanding of his policies requires not only a knowledge of their intellectual background but also a comparison with those of his predecessors— not to mention those of his possible successors. Perhaps those policies are quite new—either inspired by genius or

* From Alfred Grosser, "General de Gaulle and the Foreign Policy of the Fifth Republic," *International Affairs,* April 1963, pp. 298–313. French quotations translated. Professor Grosser's *The Foreign Policy of the Fifth Republic* published in early 1967 by Little, Brown, and Co., Boston, Mass.

characterised by aberrations. Or perhaps they differ only in tone and modes of expression from those of the Fourth Republic.

The Fourth Republic collapsed largely because France suffered what was, in comparison with other nations, a unique experience that she could well have been spared. She was the only country in the world to experience internally the anguish of the two great 20th-century conflicts: the struggle between Communism and anti-Communism and the confrontation of the old states by new nationalisms. Italy has been divided ever since the two blocs took shape. Britain has had to overcome the problems of decolonisation. But only France has suffered both internal and external conflict. The Fourth Republic might have survived if it had had the will to do so rather than allowed events to dictate its fate, and, above all, if the magnitude of the difficulties which its leaders were so often compelled to survey through the distorting mirror of internal quarrels had been understood in time.

The balance-sheet in 1958 was, indeed, far from adverse. After many hestitations, fundamental decisions had been made. Starting with the view that General de Gaulle had expressed in November 1944: "The fate of Germany is the central problem of the universe," the Fourth Republic had by then placed itself firmly in the Atlantic camp and had developed extremely friendly relations with the Federal German Republic. The unification of Europe had been born in the declaration of May 9, 1950. The signature of the Treaty of Rome in 1957 marked a new and decisive stage. The Europe of the Fourth Republic was the Europe of the Six: in 1950 MM. Robert Schuman and Jean Monnet had deliberately chosen to go ahead without Britain, and in 1954 Winston Churchill

and Anthony Eden gave only scant satisfaction to M. Mendès-France, to whom the British presence in Europe was essential. By 1958 decolonisation was well on the way to achievement. The war in Indo-China had been over for four years: Morocco and Tunisia had been independent for two years, and Black Africa knew that the *loi-cadre,* then a year old, represented but a first step towards the same goal.

But there remained Algeria: and Algeria dominated everything and explained everything, from Suez to the wave of bitter and xenophobic nationalism which swept across France and which carried in its train a deep though veiled crisis which bit deeply into the very heart of the Atlantic alliance. Thierry Maulnier's "Letter to Americans" published in *Le Figaro* on January 9, 1957, expresses the feelings which were widespread during the months which followed:

Watched by three hundred million Arabs, you have humiliated us before a Nasser. . . . You will also create a vacuum for the Russians in North Africa by taking sides against us in Algeria. Perhaps you think that after all the worst you are risking is to have to take our place? There are some French people who believe that that eventuality would not totally displease you. . . . You would perhaps be wrong to trust too much in the need we have of you. For that need is reciprocal. We cannot break the Atlantic front, but neither can you. The destruction of the ties between Europe and the United States would be the beginning not only of our end but of yours.

Yet one cannot deprive an old people which still has its pride of its only future worthy of its past without risking dragging it, perhaps against its own interests, into unpredictable passionate reactions.

France is defending *its last chance* in North Africa. Do not force it to choose between its vocation in Africa and the friendship of America.

The delivery of Anglo-American arms to Tunisia increased hostility against Britain and the United States. As anti-Communism remained no less strong, the paradoxical situation came about that the concept "No enemy except Germany" had given place, 13 years later, to something like "No friend except perhaps Germany."

General de Gaulle was borne to power on the wave of xenophobic nationalism by those groups and movements which reproached the leaders of the state for having accepted surrender and humiliation. In the summer of 1958 foreign observers were speculating about his future foreign policy. In Bonn and in Washington there was anxiety, first because the unusual is always disturbing there, and then because the Head of Government had not, in the past, shown himself to have been either especially Germanophile or particularly "European." And was not this the man who had signed a Franco-Soviet treaty in Moscow in December 1944? In London, on the other hand, there was hope that the ties between Bonn and Paris would weaken and that Franco-British relations would improve. But in London, as in Washington and Bonn, there was fear of a stronger will toward domination in Algeria.

But all these expectations were to be proved wrong. On September 14 the de Gaulle-Adenauer idyll was born. The Europe of de Gaulle was thus shown to be even more Franco-German, and even more hostile to England, than had been the Europe of Robert Schuman and Paul-Henri Spaak. In its policy towards the East, however, the Fifth Republic substituted an attitude of intransigence for the Fourth Republic's dreams of Summit Conferences. Across the Mediterranean, Algeria and Black Africa attained an independence which would have been considered criminal if it had

even been suggested in 1958. Why these surprising changes? It would be more profitable to ask if they would have been so surprising if observers had properly understood the ideas and aims of the man on whom the French were about to give their verdict in a referendum that was actually a plebiscite.

If a nationalist is defined as one who places the national idea at the top of the scale of political values, then General de Gaulle is a nationalist. A nation may be regarded as a human entity which acts in a world made up of other such entities. In this perspective, foreign policy is the only true policy. The sole aim of internal policy is to assure order and unity, and to develop an influence to be used abroad. Let us look . . . at volume III of de Gaulle's *Mémoires*. The State is not "a juxtaposition of special interests from which only weak compromises can ever emerge, but an instrument for decision, action, and ambition, expressing and serving only the national interest." When General de Gaulle recalls the social programme of his Government of 1944–1946, he notes that his aim was not that of the parties: "While they regulate their conduct according to the preconceived views of their respective political groups, these considerations affect me very little. On the contrary, I see them scarcely sensitive to the motive that inspires me which is the power of France." The same theme is discernible in his New Year Message for 1963: "Our prosperity is reaching a level that we have never before known and our social progress is making unprecedented advances. While drive and reason coupled together are restoring us to strength, France is recovering its rank, its attraction, and its means." The lot of the French is not an end, but a means to improve the destiny of France. A few sentences later he affirmed: "Progress is our national ambition today." But economic, technical and scientific progress and social progress took second place: first place was given to international progress. The message to the National Assembly on December 11, 1962, stated this equally plainly: "To continue . . . the expansion of our country . . . in such a way that there should increase at the same time the standard of living of every person, national prosperity and the power of France."

What form does this national ambition take, and what are its consequences? We are so familiar with its claims and with its contentious aspects, as they have been reflected in military, Atlantic and now European politics, that we are inclined to forget its more positive features. When, in the *Mémoires,* one comes across a sentence full of pity for the Germany of 1945: "Standard of living and reconstruction, that is what would necessarily, for many years, be the ambitions of the German nation and the goals of its policy," one is tempted, in fact, to congratulate the Germans for having been so wise. Yet have not the Americans, the English and the French for some time rebuked the Germans for being too satisfied with their standards of living and of commerce; for shunning the international responsibilities that a great industrial country ought to assume; for not doing enough for Africa? For France, at least, the provision of aid to underdeveloped countries is the logical outcome of a national ambition to play a part wherever the future of the world is being decided.

Certainly, the course of France's policy of decolonisation has been neither clear nor simple. Since 1960, when the office of President of the Community ceased to have any legal significance, the President of the Republic has shown less interest in Black Africa. Sometimes he even forgets Africa. Did he not declare in his press conference on January 14, in the presence of M. Foccart, Secretary-General to the Presidency of the Republic for the Community and for African and Malagasy Affairs, that, in contrast to Britain, not one of the Six was "tied, abroad, by any special political or military agreement"? For a long while, too, well after the proclamation of the right of the Algerians to self-determination, the Fifth Republic, like the Fourth, and contrary to the views of its Atlantic partners save Portugal, continued to assert that the war in Algeria was part of the struggle against Communism. In October 1960, for instance, the Prime Minister, M. Michel Debré, attacked M. Paul Reynaud when he declared, to the cheers of U.N.R. deputies: "To hold that we are not defending the West in Algeria is to advance the argument of our enemies."

But France's new policy towards Algeria is gradually bringing to an end the most serious rift in the history of NATO. That is what General Challe did not understand when he thought that the United States would prefer to General de Gaulle a "European" in favour both of Atlantic military integration and of *Algérie française.* Now that Algeria has gained her independence, and the problems of Atlantic integration are once again of primary importance, this is something the United States are inclined to forget.

There is also the fact that the thought of aid being given to countries which have just become independent of France is not very popular among the French. From the leftist *Le Canard Enchaîné* to the extreme Right, either for selfish reasons or from feelings of revenge, many would prefer that instructors and technicians should remain at home in France where they are needed; that attention should be given to the development of Brittany—compared with which the development of Black Africa is apparently considered more important. It is in this context that one must understand the true sense of the "national ambition" expressed by General de Gaulle in another part of his message to the Assembly which I have already quoted:

What a pressure France can, and must, exercise, in order to help solve the greatest problem in the world, the achievement of modern civilization by all people—provided that she knows how to develop her economic, technical and cultural capacity in such a way as to lend wide assistance to others and provided that her government is able to apply a coordinated and prolonged effort. How true that is especially for the States of Africa, including Algeria, toward whom our historic calling is henceforth fulfilled by cooperation.

The adverb *henceforth* needs to be emphasized. To be able to substitute decolonisation and aid for colonisation and domination as a national objective—that indeed is an extraordinary intellectual feat! One can fairly detect in this achievement a fundamental *cause* of a phenomenon which might well have surprised foreign observers even more than it has: that on the morrow of what was considered to be the supreme catastrophe—the loss of Algeria—the French people, far from being filled with bitterness, accept the ambition of creating a new French presence in Africa, and look forward to the achievement of the European Economic Community. Prosperity explains many things. But in this case the inspiration provided by the proud nationalism of General de Gaulle must also be given its due.

In the military sphere, the national ambition appears in a different light. One must distinguish here between two elements which are often confused: security and independence. The decision to build an atomic force was taken under the Fourth Republic—as a consequence of the evolution of world strategy. Ever since the Soviet Union gained the means to destroy the United States there has been no assurance that the Russians are certain that the Americans would actually risk suicide by defending Europe. This is not the place to discuss the reasons that justify (or do not justify) the existence, from the security point of view, of a French atomic force. It is enough to say that General de Gaulle has used them for his own purpose, although sometimes in a way open to criticism. The day after the Cuban crisis, all the American commentators agreed, and still agree, in saying: "the firmness of President Kennedy, a firmness which led to an unprecedented Soviet withdrawal, should prove to all Europeans that our guarantee to them is real, that we respect our commitments." In Germany, the same conclusion was drawn. For a moment, at the end of last summer, there had been a fear that Mr. Kennedy, forsaking firmness, might make a package deal in which Berlin would have been sacrificed for Cuba. The outcome of the Cuban crisis thus provided a reassurance. But General de Gaulle considered that Washington was firm over Cuba only because the Soviet bases in the island presented a direct threat to the United States. In that sense the firmness of the Americans over Cuba only proved that they would have weakened more easily over Berlin. If they had not appeared unshakable, they would have clearly shown their faintheartedness and thus their potential lack of steadfastness in Europe.

In actual fact, it is hardly likely that General de Gaulle believes in the possibility of being abandoned by the Americans. Even if the McNamara doctrine were to render Europe useless as a military base, the loss of Europe would mean total defeat for the United States in the East-West conflict. Many American commentators and political leaders actually do General de Gaulle a service when they hint that the United States may withdraw from Europe—although they themselves know it to be impossible —because they thus give the President of the Republic a reason for saying that it is possible.

But, for the President, a French nuclear force is not a purely military question. In 1934 Colonel de Gaulle saw the need for tanks not only as a military but also as a political requirement. He realised that a country with merely defensive armaments no longer possesses any diplomatic weapon with which to confront a potential adversary. The Anglo-French capitulation at Munich confirmed this point of view. The France of 1938, concentrating solely on defence, on the notion of the Maginot Line, could only say to Hitler: "Do not attack me or else . . . ," not: "Do not attack Czechoslovakia, or else . . ." Today's offensive weapon is a nuclear one. French diplomacy must therefore be backed by a French nuclear force. There can be no political independence without military independence, and political independence is a prerequisite for national ambition.

There is a seductive logic in such an attitude even if its background is a constant *hymne à la force* conspicuous in all de Gaulle's writings—from *Le Fil de l'Epée* in 1932 to his speech at the Military Academy in Hamburg in 1962. But opposed to this logic are one impossibility and two inconsistencies. The place of France in the world of 1963 cannot be that of 1939 or 1914. No political design can ignore certain fundamental facts. Not only that: the language of security and the language of independence are sometimes incompatible. Would not the security of

Europe be that much more certain if the United States were more deeply committed to Europe? Yet to the extent that they were more deeply committed the independence of Europe would be reduced. On the other hand one would have expected General de Gaulle's strategic arguments to have led to the formation of a European *force de frappe,* or at least a Franco-German one. Instead he is creating a purely national force. There is thus an inconsistency both at the Atlantic and at the European level. This inconsistency cannot be understood without taking account of another idea—an idea which has been at the root of all Atlantic and European crises even before the appearance of the Fifth Republic. It is the idea of equality.

From the day he returned to power General de Gaulle has wanted to reshape the Atlantic alliance. He has demanded equality—certainly not equality for all the members of the alliance, but, rather, that France should acquire what might be termed a superior equality through the setting up of a small group of allies, each equal with the other, but more equal than the others in the alliance, to use George Orwell's expression. The problem of equality between members of the alliance has been with us since the creation of NATO, but General de Gaulle has given it a new complexion.

The alliance has never been able to overcome certain major military and political difficulties. No doubt they are insurmountable. For instance, who should decide in an emergency? Who should decide whether there is an emergency? Everyone knows that a decision on possible use of the atomic "poker" requires precisely those conditions which, in his press conference on January 14, General de Gaulle demanded in domestic affairs: "In this action, as in all actions, there must be a head and, as that head is a person, well, it is fitting that that person should receive the personal expression of the confidence of all concerned."

But what European leader would lightheartedly hand over to a foreign Head of State—even to the President of the United States—the power of decision over the physical fate of his fellow-citizens? In the political sphere consultation and joint decisions appear more feasible, at least in theory. But in practice the United States Government, partly to avoid giving the impression to the uncommitted world that it is an accomplice of the colonial Powers, has always considered that the operational area of the alliance should be limited to that defined in the treaty. Thus there has never been any joint policy for Laos or Cuba, for the Congo or the Yemen, although the term "Atlantic Community" has been continually used in those contexts. In effect the alliance has always been characterised by an Orwellian equality.

The prime objective of Gaullist policy since 1958 has therefore been to join the "super-equals." But perhaps one may wonder if such a group really exists. Does Britain have a privileged place in the alliance in relation to the United States? Has she ever been consulted to a greater extent than the other allies? However the military and political analysts may answer these questions, General de Gaulle's replies to both are in the affirmative. Britain *is* privileged. France must correct this situation by securing at least the same status in the alliance. The *force de frappe* represents one way of achieving that status although one cannot see what advantage Britain's nuclear weapons have ever given her over France—at the time of the Suez crisis, for instance). Support from Germany provides another means to the same end. Why should a *rap-*

prochement between London and Paris in 1958 have replaced the *entente* with Bonn, given the fact that the latter was designed to help France to improve her position *vis-à-vis* Great Britan through co-operation with the Federal Republic which had never aspired to play a leading role in the alliance, and so could not be considered in any way a rival? Here is a clear indication of the French objective: not to abandon the alliance, as some feared, and to attempt to play the impossible role of arbiter between East and West, but to use the Federal German Republic as an aid to achieve for France an enhanced "rank" in the Atlantic Community. And if it be asked why Chancellor Adenauer's Germany should be content with a secondary role to France in the Alliance, the answer is to be found in the fact that she receives French support in the East.

Not enough attention may have been paid to one surprising fact—that General de Gaulle, who of all French statesmen ought to be the most inclined to favour a policy of appeasement of the Soviet Union, has proved to be more intransigent toward Moscow than his predecessors. Indeed, his conception of international character, based more on nations than on ideologies, has led him to refer more often to Russia than to the Soviet Union. France and Russia are, as he said to Mr. Khrushchev when he was last in Paris, "daughters of the same Europe." If every French Government since 1947 has lived in hope of a Summit Conference it is because a relaxation of tension has seemed to be in France's interest. Why? Because whenever there has been tension between East and West, the attractions of the Federal German Republic have increased in the eyes of the United States while dissension has grown in France, where, as the Pentagon knew, a quarter of the electors voted Communist. On the other hand, when tension relaxed, Federal Germany relapsed into the role of a pawn on the international chessboard while France again became one of the Big Four discussing the German problem. If the Paris agreements were accepted by the Senate in 1955, it was because M. Edgar Faure had convinced the Senators that their ratification would be more likely to lead to a Summit Conference than their rejection. General de Gaulle, in contrast, in his concern for the status of France, has repeatedly demanded firmness on the part of the West against the East and has only once consented to a Summit Conference—when it was agreed that it would be held in Paris under his aegis with no chance of achieving anything practical.

The first reason for this attitude is psychological: one does not yield under pressure, one does not yield when one is weak. When, during the war, Churchill asked him to be more flexible with Roosevelt, de Gaulle replied that he had not got the British Empire behind him, and that this weakness compelled him to be intransigent. Twenty years later, in a speech on television, he began by expatiating at length on the wealth and strength of France, not forgetting the milk from her cows and the meat from her cattle. He then announced the beginning of negotiations with the FLN. A strong and prosperous country which is willing to negotiate thereby gives proof of her generosity; for a weak country, negotiation is capitulation. In any eventual negotiations over Germany the West would be obliged to make unilateral concessions—for in all the three problems under discussion (the Oder-Neisse line, Berlin and recognition of the German Democratic Republic) any change in the *status quo* would amount to withdrawal by the West, particularly if the Polish-German frontier is regarded

as unalterable. Negotiation must therefore be avoided.

The second and main reason for firmness is the priority given by General de Gaulle to the alliance with Germany. This firmness does not rule out a simultaneous if sorrowful attitude to the East which is tempered by the hope, even by the certainty, of an evolution of the Soviet Union. The U.S.S.R., whether she likes it or not, has in fact already joined the "haves," while China is taking her place as the leader of the "have nots." The first point of *action extérieure,* defined in the message of December 11, reads thus:

In the face of the totalitarian system drawn up against the West, social liberty, equality and fraternity, sought by means of the collectivity's economic and cultural progress and by the action of an equitable and vigorous state, are in fact needed, not only to assure the unity of the nation but still more to offer the other camp the striking and attractive demonstration of a way of life which is more fruitful than theirs and to hasten that transformation in them, that has perhaps already begun, which is the true chance of peace.

Once Russia becomes more liberal the free world will, of course, no longer retain its present shape, and it will be possible to escape from American protection with a sigh of relief. To speak, as the President did in the same message, of "the Atlantic Alliance which at the moment is necessary to the defense of the free world" is to envisage not the destruction of the Alliance in the face of a "totalitarian" Soviet Union, but rather its uselessness in face of a Russia in which Communism has been transformed. Yet so long as this vision (or this dream) does not become a reality, it is necessary to fight for Orwellian equality *vis-à-vis* a necessary but little-loved America at the centre of the alliance. The combination of the desire for "rank" in the alliance and the hope of a disappearance of the Soviet threat results in apparently contradictory behaviour: the French consider themselves less blindly anti-Communist than the United States, but they resent any kind of agreement between the two Ks.[1] An agreement with Russia is acceptable only if it does not conjure up the memory of a conference at Yalta in which France did not take part. A direct agreement between the Big Two is to be condemned because a peace so established could be a peace in which the United States and the U.S.S.R. dominated the world. The threat of such domination is removed if the two become three by being joined, if not by France, at least by Europe.

Nobody can henceforth conceal from himself the deep worry that the future of the relations between America and Russia imposes on the destiny of every country and of every individual. Who then can restore the balance, other than the old world between the two new worlds? Old Europe which, for so many centuries, was the guide of the universe, is capable of providing, in the heart of a world which is tending to cut itself in two, the necessary element of compensation and comprehension. The nations of the classical West . . . resolved to preserve an independence that would be gravely endangered in case of a conflagration, physically and morally related both to the collective effort of the Russians and to the liberal drive of the Americans, globally powerful because of their own resources and those of the vast territories that are bound to their destiny, extending far and wide their influence and their activities, what pressure those nations might exert if they could succeed in co-ordinating their policies, in spite of their age-old quarrels.

That was what General de Gaulle said at Bar-le-Duc on July 28, 1946. He added: "Such a harmony implies first of

all understanding between London and Paris." It is true that at a press conference on March 16, 1950, commenting on Chancellor Adenauer's initiative, he said: "If one did not compel oneself to look at things coldly, one would be almost dazzled by the perspective of what could be produced together by the worth of Germany and the worth of France, the latter extended by Africa." But two months later the Europe based on Franco-German accord, and destined to become a respected partner of the United States, was set up by the very men whom the General was opposing on account of their defeatist attitude, the men who attack him today for pursuing policies which they themselves were then supporting.

To General de Gaulle, the "Europeans" in France were weak because, without hope of restoring the internal situation and the international status of France, they took refuge in the European idea. To some extent he has gone in the same direction since his return to office. To him Europe is not just an instrument of French *grandeur,* but rather a new political entity in which France must certainly play a decisive role, an entity which, at the same time, is acquiring the individual characteristics of a nation. Thus the concept of Europe remains ambiguous, and the ambiguity can clearly be seen in the inconsistencies over political unification. General de Gaulle has accepted the European Economic Community. The monetary reform of December 1958 in France has made possible a more enthusiastic and an effective French co-operation in the Community than had previously seemed likely. The Gaullists had fought violently against the Community, but there are several reasons why they no longer regard it as an issue. In the first place, the Fifth Republic, being by definition

[1] Kennedy and Krushchev.—Ed.

a strong State, can afford attitudes which would have been considered defeatist in a weak country. Secondly, the Community is regarded as merely an economic experiment, and thus of secondary importance. But, third and most important, the Community reinforces the power of the *Europe des Six,* and so it can be used to achieve the political ends I have already described.

In such a context General de Gaulle's hostility to Britain's entry to the Community can be traced to two distinct but related reasons. On the one hand, Britain does not accept the concept of economic unity: she merely sees the Community as a Free Trade Area. Even if Britain accepted the Community in its present form, she would obstruct further progress within it toward greater economic unity in terms of a common budget, currency and social policy, co-ordination of investments and economic planning on the French pattern. On the other hand, Britain would prevent Europe, both deliberately and as a means of curbing any move toward greater unity, from achieving a separate identity in the Western world. General de Gaulle said at his press conference on January 14 [1963]: "It is a different Common Market whose construction one would have to envisage. . . . Definitively, there would appear a colossal Atlantic Community under American dependence and leadership which would soon have absorbed the Community of Europe."

But there is an inconsistency here which must have been the secret despair of the French negotiators in Brussels. Ostensibly their intransigence toward Great Britain was based on the same argument as was used by the Hallstein Commission: that the Treaty of Rome was not only economic in character but had a political objective. It was intended that the Community should, by preliminary economic means, ultimately achieve political unity—through the creation, in one form or another, of a political authority which would make its decisions by majority vote. Yet General de Gaulle does not want such an authority. He is therefore opposing Britain's entry in the name of a Europe which he himself rejects. It matters little at present whether the Germans (excepting the Chancellor), the Belgians or the Italians still support the idea of a supranational political authority: the French diplomatists are entangled in a contradiction from which they can only extricate themselves by admitting a reality which is inadmissible.

General de Gaulle dislikes impersonal international or supranational organisations, even those dominated by a single personality—such bodies as the Secretariat-General of the United Nations, that of NATO and the High Authority of the Coal and Steel Community. Nor, doubtless, would he like the Hallstein Commission if it thought of taking decisions. He dislikes, no less, Assemblies which by their nature are both demagogic and verbose: the U.N. General Assembly, the European Assembly, the French National Assembly. General de Gaulle believes rather in directorates, of differing size, but all based on power: five for the United Nations, three for NATO, two for Europe, one in France. The Benelux leaders are not wholly mistaken in fearing that the Europe of the Six might be dominated by the Franco-German partnership.

There is no reason to believe, however, that Franco-German relations are likely to deteriorate rapidly following the rupture at Brussels, or as a result of the Chancellor's retirement. Certainly Dr. Adenauer's successors, whoever they may be, are likely to reject an exclusive union with France and to be more "polygamous." Moreover, General de Gaulle is mistaken if he thinks that the Federal

Republic would support him against the United States, as he is also mistaken in thinking that the Benelux countries and Italy would submit to Franco-German domination as an alternative to American domination. But the fact is that present relations between France and the Federal Republic, in large part the result of much unobserved work since 1945, are based on a kind of human infrastructure which is independent of political circumstances—a fact giving them a special character which, in turn, accounts for many aspects of the treaty signed in Paris on January 22, 1963. A check made at the end of January showed public opinion in France hesitant about the policy adopted toward Great Britain (40 per cent. in favour, 21 per cent. not in favour, 39 per cent. did not answer) but very much in favour of the Franco-German treaty (61 per cent. in favour, 14 per cent. against and 25 per cent. did not answer).

The real question posed by the rupture at Brussels concerns not so much the nature and content of General de Gaulle's policy as the reasons for his attitude. Why did he not, as it seems M. Couve de Murville suggested to him that he should, resort to gentler, if more hypocritical, methods to bring about a breakdown in the negotiations? One explanation could be found in the wish to be brutal when weak. To him it must have seemed that the success of the negotiations was inevitable, and that only some dramatic act or utterance could torpedo them. A second explanation is more likely, although not to the complete exclusion of the first. Maybe General de Gaulle wanted to treat his partners in the EEC rather like he treats the political forces in France, and that with this object he manoeuvred, as would a good strategist, with no trace of sentiment. As there can be no Europe without France the five, disappointed and

rebellious though they might be, would face the alternative of allowing the EEC to collapse or, despite their fury, of continuing its development. As de Gaulle needed the Common Market the risk was considerable. He must have calculated that, as the interest of the five was in the continuing development of the EEC, they would accept the situation. But he has thus shown a complete and fundamental lack of understanding of what could be called the European spirit. Even if the five overcome their indignation at the way in which the rupture in Brussels was brought about, they quite rightly considered methods of power politics traditionally used against opponents as inappropriate between members of the same Community.

A contempt for people and a taste for *realpolitik* have combined to make General de Gaulle commit his first political error—if the definition of a political error is that it is an act which runs counter to the desired objective. The Community of the Six is likely to be affected for a long time by the blow it has suffered from the man who wanted to defend it, even against its former champions such as Paul-Henri Spaak, Jean Monnet and the United States Government, who are today supporting a very different Europe.

An offended and aggressive Britain; an American press highly suspicious of the real aims of French policy; an irritated and distressed German ally; four other members of the European Coal and Steel Community shocked and humiliated. Whether or not these reactions are superficial or deeprooted, they exist; they have been provoked by General de Gaulle and they feature in today's balance sheet of the foreign policy of the Fifth Republic. But to say that is not enough, any more than it would be enough merely to claim that there is a credit balance—on the grounds that negative prestige is still prestige, and that General de Gaulle occupies the forefront of the political stage as has no French leader since the end of the war, with the exception of M. Mendès-France. The real items on the balance sheet are to be found elsewhere.

The first point to be made, and one almost forgotten by all French and foreign commentators, is that this difficult, proud man, who never ceases to boast of his eccentricity, whose unpredictability is forever being asserted, has hitherto respected all the fundamental decisions made, frequently in opposition to his views, by the Fourth Republic. From the North Atlantic Treaty to the Franco-German *rapprochement,* from decolonisation to the desire to build the Europe of the Six, the situation created by his predecessors has been maintained by General de Gaulle and, on the whole, reinforced. In fact there has been no less continuity than when a Republican administration has been followed by a Democrat administration in the United States, or when a Conservative government has been followed by a Labour government in Britain—although there has been a change of régime, and although decisions which were formerly laboriously worked out against the background of complex and differing points of view have been replaced by those representing the will of one lonely man.

The tone has certainly changed. So has the style. Now, as in the past, there is the aim to give France prosperity, a good standard of life, social justice. But what was as a rule the primary objective of the past has become, at least as far as the Head of State is concerned, an internal means to an external end. Abroad there have been developments which have affected, but not really changed, the situation in France. Thus the Franco-

German hatchet has been buried very much more successfully than was the case in 1958 even if, for General de Gaulle, it implies a new relationship between the *Gaulois* and the *Germains,* a happy sequel to Jacques Bainville's *Histoire de deux Peuples,* rather than a mere accord between a democratic France and a Germany freed from the taint of Nazism. In Africa and the Near East the standing of France has considerably improved, thanks to the conclusion of the Algerian war. The allies of France may have had their faith in her shaken, but no more than it was in September 1954 on the morrow of the rejection of the European Defence Community. Yet other facts could be cited, but they are not essential to the argument.

The choices before France have remained the same; only the method of dealing with them has changed. What are France's objectives? Perhaps the choices before her are only superficialy similar, for what may appear to be the objective in one case may be merely the means to an end in another. Is the Atlantic option a first step toward a Community or merely a temporary means of ensuring the defence of France? Is Europe to provide France with a means of asserting her position or is it to be a new political unit in which national independence will gradually be submerged? Atomic weapons—are they means which are reluctantly chosen because they are necessary in a particular strategic situation or are they an essential part of French independence? One is tempted to conclude that there is a profound difference between the objectives of the Fourth Republic and the Fifth. But such a conclusion would be superficial. In fact, the Fourth Republic had no clear and coherent objectives; nor has the Fifth. There is more clarity and coherence, however, in General de Gaulle's policy which makes it shocking to a world in which contradictory objectives are the norms of international life.

De Gaulle wants peace, but not peace in its most obvious form, that of agreement between the two Great Powers. He wants security, a security guaranteed by France herself, but in his atomic calculations he needs to take account of the American nuclear force. He wants "Europe," but a Europe capable of taking a decisive part in the shaping of world events. The objectives of the Fourth Republic were much less clear. More precisely, they included both those of General de Gaulle and others completely opposed to them—an Atlantic Community, even if dominated by the Americans, and an integrated Europe composed of equal members. De Gaulle criticises his predecessors for their inconsistencies, or rather for the fact that their "national" objectives were no more than talk. For their part his opponents attack what they regard as his lack of realism. But in fact General de Gaulle is now proving by his policy that, with few exceptions, practically no nation today can have a foreign policy founded upon a clear-cut choice between national and ideological interest.

After the end of the war, Stalin made an astonishing discovery: that Communist leaders of countries other than the Soviet Union could find it difficult to reconcile their Communism and their specific national interests which differed from those of other Communist countries, of which the Soviet Union was one. Stalin found the remedy—which failed in Yugoslavia: suppression of the contradiction by force. In the Western world, the absence of brute force between allies emphasises the existence of a similar contradiction. For the United States and the Federal Republic there is no contradiction in their policies. In the United States ideological and national interests have always been identical. In Western Germany the defence of the most pressing national interest, Berlin, is simultaneously a prominent issue in the ideological conflict between East and West. What is more, the great majority of the Germans have, consciously or unconsciously, made what is, in the Western Alliance, quite an exceptional decision: they prefer that their country should be divided rather that there should be the slightest risk of its Western part being infected by Communism.

But for other countries there can be no simple choice between national and ideological interests, between national separatism and the unity of a civilisation which both Europe and the Atlantic nexus are perhaps on the way to creating. The choice would undoubtedly be easier if the Atlantic Community were composed of equals, but it is not and cannot be. Look at British reactions to the cancellation of Skybolt. Look at Canadian reactions when faced with American atomic demands. How right they showed de Gaulle to be! Yet how wrong he is if the essential objective is really the defence of a common freedom!

To be sure, the points made in this article do not make it any easier to predict the day-to-day policy of General de Gaulle; nor do they necessarily lead one to approve or disapprove any particular position he may take up. But they may induce a more calm and more careful judgment of the foreign policy of the Fifth Republic, a policy which reflects the desire to introduce the absolute into a world where only the relative corresponds with reality.

In *Seven Times Seven Days* (1947), Resistance leader EMMANUEL D'ASTIER (1900–   ), presents in the form of diary extracts from the war years one of the most penetrating vignettes of de Gaulle as a wartime leader. In the following extract, d'Astier describes his first meeting with de Gaulle, when he agreed to go to Washington on behalf of the Free French, and the unusual circumstances in which he became Commissioner of the Interior in the French Committee of National Liberation in Algiers.*

► ||||| *Great, Cold Prelate*

London, 12th May [1942]
"You'll dine with him tonight at nine o'clock."

I went there at nine.

It was at the Connaught Hotel, the most exquisitely old-fashioned of hotels in London. A porter, as padded as the carpets and the lift, led me to an empty drawing-room where a table was laid for two.

I stood waiting. Symbole came in.

He's even taller than one expects.

His movements are slow and heavy like his nose. His small head and waxen face are carried on a body of indeterminate structure. His most habitual gesture is to raise his forearms while keeping his elbows to his side. At these moments, his inert, very white, rather feminine

hands, their palms turned downwards and attached to his arms by too-slender wrists, seem to be raising a whole world of abstract burdens.

He asked me no questions. We dined.

He does not love his fellow men: he loves their history, above all the history of France, in which he is acting a chapter that he seems to be writing concurrently in his head, like an impassioned Michelet.

As for me, traveller and seeker that I am, I said things which were either much too precise or much too confused, in which were mingled concrete details and Utopian sentiments. He gathered up only odds and ends here and there and put them in his history.

As with the others this morning, I had

* From Emmanuel d'Astier, *Seven Times Seven Days,* translated by Humphrey Hare (London: MacGibbon & Kee Ltd., 1958), pp. 72–73, 75–76, 123–125, 127–130, 132–133.

so great an impression of insurmountable incredulity—that incredulity in which I have been living in France for the last eighteen months as if in a cloud of cotton-wool—that I pleaded both his cause and our own. But why should he be incredulous? Suspicious, yes, because he despises men too much and too many things in the universe. Incredulous, no, because I am a French ant bringing him a fragment of straw, a piece of material for his history about which revolves a world of supernumerary friends and enemies, as Henri, Charles, Isabeau and Calixte revolve about Jeanne in a phrase-book.

I came out with my head in a whirl.

I had been in a theatre of history; I wanted to go out into life, my life.

London, 29th May [1942]
Have I done well to accept?

I shall be a month late, and I shall have several hours of torments wondering whether my decision is due to Symbole's pressing call or to a shameful desire for a respite from danger.

This evening I was suddenly summoned to see him.

He was tired. He rakes up past historical events such as Fashoda. Though he is leader only of a handful of men and a few distant territories, his enemies and his pride have combined to make him so conscious of greatness that he speaks as if he bore the weight of a thousand years of history or as if he saw himself living a hundred years ago. He paints a sombre picture of his Calvary—that of France in his person. And I thought suddenly that he only gives way to his dark fervour in order to encourage the genius of France and to restore her national and historic fire, the only fire in which he believes.

Does he suffer from the same inability as his entourage? The persons around him were awaiting more from the man than from France. While seeking victory they failed to see the prize that the people—who alone pay and lose—wish to win, and which is not only a matter of history and geography.

Surely not! Yet, having garnered so much wisdom from folly, he can see only empiricism. He feels that he embodies the nation so well that he forgets men and the immediate present, the incoherence, the necessary Utopian folly, and that distant future called humanity. How can one make it clear to him: one cannot argue with a symbol about what he symbolizes?

He asked me to go to America to plead his cause, our cause. And I can imagine him, if he saw the phrase I have written, slowly shrugging his shoulders and saying: "His cause, our cause: there is no such thing, it is the cause of France."

Very well: I shall go.

Algiers, November 18th, 19th, 1943

On the fifth day—when I was already beginning to become very bored—I was summoned to see Symbole.

Once again, as happens every time I meet him, I was seized with embarrassment. In order not to succumb to it. I arrived with notes, without which I am in danger of yielding to his hypnosis, and saying "yes" . . . "yes" to his great tirades on the malice of nations and the meanness of men.

I started to voice the complaints of the Resistance. He gave me my head and then suddenly interrupted me with a phrase I shall never remember precisely but which was in essence: "Leave all that, let's talk of serious matters. I'm setting up a Government, you must take the Ministry of the Interior . . . And then you'll be able to give them all they need, because it will be entirely your responsibility. . . ."

He was sitting on a sofa. His expression was slightly ironical and contemptuous; his heavy eyelids seemed to press his eyes down towards the carpet and the corners of the room, while his head rolled impatiently on his neck. I could not catch his eye and I replied: "No."

"Why not?"

I put forward my arguments, which were either conditions or eventual objections. He agreed to the former and waved away the latter. He demurred only when I said that I wanted to return to France in February or March. Then he yielded, because it still seemed to him to be a long way off and perhaps because he was convinced of what he had stated a moment before: "The war is over, it's now no more than a formality." And he painted for me a rapid picture, as epic as a funeral oration, of our approaching landing in France and of all the tasks that awaited us, producing it all as if it were wine with which to intoxicate me.

I asked him for two days in which to think it over: he gave me six hours. It was an 18th Brumaire with which to confront the Allies, and time was short.

What should I do? I have no friends or counsellors. There is no time to get a reply from my comrades in France. Boris, who is rather like Father Joseph —a pessimistic and perspicacious political critic—says: "Accept." Morandat says the same. These are all the counsellors I have; I know no one else whom I can trust.

I went off alone into the sunshine. Unable to play the devil's advocate for long, I yielded to that spiritual bent which turns life into a novel and, through the processes of the imagination, induces one to act it.

At nine o'clock in the evening, I went back to see Symbole. Première Personne went in to see him first. He appears to be the very incarnation of energy, both in voice and gesture; but one suddenly wonders whether he has not laboured for years to arrive where he is and whether he has not exhausted all his energy in the process.

The atmosphere was sepulchral and there was a long pause: Symbole was sitting in the shadow. I don't remember that he said three words. Perhaps I talked of my conditions, my scruples and my acceptance. I was so concerned at what was happening to me that I was not even astonished by the secrecy with which he surrounds all his actions, and the fact that he had not told me any of his dispositions. He did not ask me a single question, nor did he seek or give advice, or reveal any of his intentions. He is like some great, cold prelate whose kingdom is France, a kingdom not perhaps of this world, and which he will share with no one. We are but choirboys: when I asked him if Première Personne was accepting a portfolio, he said: "Yes." But he was thinking of something else: he was in a hurry and absent-minded. On the chess-board on which he plays, there can be no friendship between the knight that is moved and the hand that moves it. I felt that he placed no value upon us except the one he was giving us. And that no one was indispensable, except himself. Tonight, the King of Bourges, playing in Algiers, was preparing a gambit....

On Tuesday morning, I opened the newspapers to try to find some infomation concerning the Government of which I am a member. There was nothing, but I was summoned to the Glycines. Symbole was looking annoyed, with the sideways glance of a child who is up to no good. Instead of telling me the truth straight out and explaining the difficulty he was in, he entangled himself in a lie: "You told me that you would join my Government whatever the post, whatever the conditions."

"No!"

I kept my temper and explained that had only accepted the portfolio in order to accomplish a particular task for the benefit of my comrades, one which he himself had defined. I reminded him how pertinently he had shown me that I could not refuse this task, and with what ease he had demolished my objections and accepted my conditions.

He relinquished his tortuous approach and asked me to accept the Ministry of Information. He flaunted his new merchandise: if he was to be believed, Interior and Information were practically the same thing. He so blundered in his role of President du Conseil of the Third Republic that I was embarrassed. I put an end to the scene by telling him of my relief at not having to leave my comrades and of my intention of returning to London tomorrow morning and to Paris as soon as possible. We were now both on our feet and he grew angry, playing at being the General. Knowing that he hates revealing his tactics, a commander's privilege, I asked him why he had changed his mind.

"I can't give you the Interior: there are too many people against it." He metioned them by name: Saint-Bernard and Piétinant. We parted without shaking hands. When I reached the door, he called me back: "Come to Fromentin at midday . . ." Fromentin is the seat of the Council. I repeated that I had no intention of changing my mind. He insisted: "Come at midday, the Council will be over. I want to talk to you before you leave."

I accepted. I had never been so relieved in my life. I rushed off to Melamel at the Vieux-Palais and argued so successfully that I obtained the promise of a seat in an aircraft to London the following morning.

That seemed to be the end of the story. I had had a good time and would have no account to render my comrades. I wandered from shop to shop, looking for souvenirs which would not encumber me too much. I filled my pockets with those cigarettes called "Cream of the Divine Herb," which had delighted me when, disguised as a British major, I was in Algiers in July, having been set down there in error, and while waiting for an aircraft to take me to France.

At half-past twelve, I went to Fromentin to say goodbye to Symbole. On the porch, Joxe, the Secretary-General, was fussing about.

"You're very late. They're waiting for you . . ."

"What do you mean? Have they finished already?"

"No. They're waiting for you to go in to the meeting, your place is empty."

I explained to him the morning's scene and my approaching departure.

He raised his hands to heaven.

"But the General's waiting for you, what can I tell him?"

"That I've come to say goodbye to him, as he asked me to do."

"But there's an empty chair. They're a minister short. It doesn't make sense."

"A minister of what? Of the Interior or of Information?"

"I'll go and see."

The farce went on for some five minutes. Aurion, a comrade from France, came up to me and said kindly but confusingly: "This is intolerable. We're all agreed. You must accept." Joxe kept on running in to whisper to Symbole and coming out again to try to persuade me, but without enlightening me. I gazed out across the Bay of Algiers and

at that vegetation which I dislike because it isn't alive, particularly when the
heat does not excuse its existence. I
grew stubborn. I had no faith in the
situation and was greatly tempted to return to France.

"Come on, come in. He says that
everything'll be arranged."

"I very much want to leave, but I
won't go back on my promise: if the
General accepts the conditions I made
on Sunday and if the post is that of the
Minister of the Interior, I'll come in . . ."

A minute later, Joxe came back.
His face, which never betrays emotion,
looked just a little pinker.

"It's agreed. Quick. It's nearly over."
. . . Thus, in three days, I have seen him
make unequal use of his three weapons:
prestige, secrecy and cunning. His cunning is mediocre, but his secrecy, supported by a natural, icy prestige, takes
him a long way. I have often wondered
what his prestige derives from: his
height? . . . Or from his appearance,
which is always so typical of himself,
like a portrait of himself, a picture showing a lack of sensitivity to the warmth
of life? Or from his inspired voice, its
broken cadences emerging from an in-
animate body lacking in all animal

warmth, a voice issuing from a waxwork?
Or from his aloofness from his fellow
men? Or from his language, always too
infallible even when his thought is not,
approximating in certain of his utter-
ances to the great sermons of the eigh-
teenth century? Or from his remoteness,
his expressionless body and his few ges-
tures which, in the last analysis, are as
solemn and inevitable as his adjectives?
. . . I do not know. He remains a mystery: this man, motivated by one historical idea, the greatness of France, and
whose single voice seems to replace all
others, the voice of God, man, progress
and all ideologies. How I regret not
having known him before or, rather,
during the course of those few days at
the end of June and the beginning of
July, 1940, during which he incarnated
France. Then he departed, a controversial figure, a Plutarchian character in
search of an historical role, which he had
then not yet found . . . He left to make
an epic gesture. What internal voice
must he have heard night and morning,
on awakening, while shaving, eating,
dressing, so that a month later he should
have raised, clothed and nourished
France?

One of the shrewdest and most scintillating of the many protests raised after de Gaulle's veto on Britain's Common Market membership was Nora Beloff's *The General Says No.* NORA BELOFF, after graduating from Oxford where her brother Max is Gladstone Professor of Government and Public Administration, worked in the French section of the Political Intelligence Department of the British government. As a journalist after the war, she was in Reuters' Paris office at the end of the first de Gaulle regime, and later represented *The Manchester Guardian, The Economist,* and *The Observer,* for whom she covered the negotiations on Britain's EEC candidature. Among the "many unsolved mysteries" of that time, she felt, was the character of de Gaulle. In this extract, she develops one of d'Astier's brief asides to show that de Gaulle's character traits are often the unsuspected explanation of his policies.*

► | | | | **Enigma**

Few people can have studied the de Gaulle phenomenon with more attention than the General himself. He is that rare specimen: a man who invented his own character. He can almost be seen staggering under the weight of a legendary superman whom he himself created for the glory of France and de Gaulle.

Is there still, hidden somewhere inside this incredible artefact, a real person with pity for his fellow men, an occasional urge for pleasure, and a mortal's fear of death? No one will ever know. The man whom the President of France so often refers to in the third person, whose place in history (as he once told Duff Cooper) he takes a little time off each day to examine, and who corresponds so neatly with his own youthful vision of the hero-martyr-patriot—this is the only de Gaulle the world will be allowed to see.

It is sometimes supposed that this archaic figure (is it by chance that his presidential office in the Élysée is decorated by a classical tapestry of Don Quixote?), brought up as he was in a highly conventional army family, was no more than a small-town provincial officer without any real contact with the intellectual ferment of his time. On the contrary, though it is true that his philosophical curiosity was satisfied early in life, and that he rarely absorbs ideas produced after the First World War, he

* From Nora Beloff, *The General Says No: Britain's Exclusion from Europe* (London: Penguin Books Ltd., 1963), pp. 19–26.

comes from a distinguished and intellectually eminent family, with judges, historians, teachers, and writers among his forebears. . . .

The mystique of the nation-state as the supreme repository of human endeavour, and its counterpart, the need for its embodiment in a single leader, was not an idea invented by the General. He grew up when jingoism was at its zenith and made respectable by high-sounding philosophical doctrines. In the words of his wartime Minister of the Interior, Emmanual d'Astier, whose brief biography of the General is perhaps the best, de Gaulle "was to make of Nietzsche, Charles Maurras, and Machiavelli a very personal salad."

There is obviously a good deal of Nietzsche in the superman de Gaulle created and became. Yet his orthodox Catholic upbringing and convictions always made it impossible for him to accept the cult of physical violence and totalitarianism adopted by other Nietzsche disciples. His first book, *Discord among our Enemies,* written partly during his two years as a German prisoner-of-war and published in 1924, attributed the defeat of the German leaders to their acceptance of Nietzsche's theories of an élite to whom everything —"violence, passions, personal ambition"— is allowed. De Gaulle instead counselled moderation and restraint, praising the perfections of a French garden with its geometric harmonies and *"le sens de l'équilibre, du possible, de la mesure."*[1]

It was already plain that the arbitrary tyranny of the Nazis would repel him: he was never among those French right-wingers who, in the thirties, were sucked into the extremist factions. Charges of

"Fascism" levelled against him both during the war and more recently have always been wholly unjust.

His association with Charles Maurras, the second-ingredient of his salad, was more complicated. He certainly owed more to the French philosopher of absolutism, the men who castigated the Republic as *"la gueuse"* (the harlot), than to any other thinker. From Maurras he took the idea of the *"pays réel,"* to which patriotism is due, as a separate phenomenon from the *"pays légal,"* the country expressed in its existing institutions. In the famous first sentence of his *Memoirs—"Toute ma vie je me suis fait une certaine idée de la France"*[2]— he is manifestly talking of the *pays réel:* an infinite splendour, quite detached from the *pays légal,* the old Third Republic he despised.

Also from Maurras comes the deep monarchial strain in de Gaulle's thinking: the idea of the chief, above party politics, embodying the whole nation. The General remains to this day convinced that the French people, despite their revolutions and reigns of terror, are basically monarchist, and that they respond best not to the tyranny of a demagogue who depends on plebiscites and passion, but to the staid control of a monarch whom they feel incarnates their collective personality. Looking back on June 1940, de Gaulle was able to write: *"En ce moment, le pire de son histoire, c'était à moi d'assumer la France,"*—it was my task, at this moment, the worst in her history, to take France over. Since then, the General has thought of himself as a reigning monarch. The Fourth Republic was endorsed many times over by the French electorate, but for de Gaulle it was al-

[1] "The sense of balance, of the possible, of moderation."—Ed.

[2] "All my life I have conceived a particular idea of France."—Ed.

ways a régime of usurpers until, in May 1958, Charles was restored to his throne.

Yet, though mentally attuned to Maurras, de Gaulle was too good a Catholic to support h'm once his totalitarian views brought him into collision with the Vatican. Indeed there is only one prewar incident on record when the future general did get himself involved in a political fight. This was when he accepted an invitation from the intellectual wing of the Maurras Movement, the Cercle Fustel de Coulange, to repeat, in a Sorbonne lecture-hall, talks on the role of the army which he had first delivered at the War College. In glorifying *"l'esprit militaire"* as vital to the nation, de Gaulle offended the pacifist and left-wing leanings of a large part of the student body. [Georges] Cattaui, the General's preferred biographer, writes: "The success of these talks produced unfortunate repercussions and, as a result of disturbances and interruptions, the lectures had to be suspended."

It was in 1932, the year of his most famous book, *Fil de l'Épée,* that de Gaulle revealed the third, Machiavellian ingredient of his salad: the ideal of a prince who is free from the normal bonds of conscience and who requires, in that unforgettable Gaullist phrase, *"une forte dose d'égoïsme, d'orgueil, de dureté, et de ruse."* All these four qualities have been developed to their limits by the General, during his two spells of power.

Égoïsme: The *"Moi, Général de Gaulle"* (first introduced to France by the B.B.C. during the war) is, in the General's view, the incarnation of France, which is the most important country of the most important continent in the world. Not for de Gaulle the "cowardly modesty" he notes in lesser men. The General indeed has never

hesitated to compare himself with the greatest figures of French history—Joan of Arc, Louis XIV, Napoleon, Clemenceau—unperturbed by the sardonic laughter evoked by these comparisons, especially the first. Once when some misguided visitors to the Élysée dared to refer to the General's predecessors, thinking of the former occupants of the presidential palace, he cut in: *"Messieurs, sachez que de Gaulle n'a pas de prédécesseurs!"*[3] On one of his tours of the French provinces local notabilities told him that as long as he was their leader, they had nothing to fear: but what would come after? "France," they were told, "must find another de Gaulle." It is precisely this egoism which has been such a boon to satirists and mimics the world over. It would be a poor dinner party in Paris these days if none of the guests was capable of raising a laugh by a recognizable imitation of the "supreme guide."

Orgueil: The General's pride shows itself in a most inconvenient form, in his daily conduct of state business. He never asks to see anyone. If anyone wishes to see him, they may seek an audience. The result is that some very important Frenchmen, politicians, businessmen, labour leaders, have never been admitted to the Élysée at all.

The General is too proud to ask for what he wants. Everyone knows how strongly he feels that France must have its own nuclear striking force. He is not unnaturally resentful that nuclear secrets, shared by the United States and Britain, and certainly known to the Russians, are withheld from France. Millions of pounds and years of research are today being wasted by the French

[3] "Gentlemen, you should know that de Gaulle has no predecessors!"—Ed.

Treasury while France repeats the whole process of nuclear research. It is fairly clear in retrospect, and it is confirmed by senior members of the Élysée staff, that what the General wanted from the British during recent European discussions was an offer of nuclear partnership which would have allowed the two countries to share their knowledge and work together. Whether or not this was the best way of serving Western interests, the idea would certainly have evoked considerable sympathy from the British Government, which shared the General's own belief in a national nuclear deterrent. There is reason to believe that if he had come forward with a specific proposal, even if it had involved renegotiating Britain's agreements with the United States, it would have received the Prime Minister's careful attention. The General, however, felt he must not demean himself by indicating what he wanted.

Dureté: Anyone who works closely with the General is always astonished by his indifference to the well-being of even his most fervent supporters. He has a manifest contempt for his own Cabinet ministers: they can be seen squirming with embarrassment over decisions he has taken without asking their advice and has then left them to carry out. Michel Debré, who, in the days of Gaullist opposition, frequently and publicly declared that any politician who separated Algeria from France would be guilty of high treason, was Prime Minister when the General decided to accept the rebel Algerian demand for total independence. Debré entreated the General to let him resign. "No, Debré," the General is reported to have said. "I need you." Later, when Debré was not needed any more, he was dismissed without even the support he required to preserve

his seat in Parliament, which he accordingly lost at the next general election.

Again, it was Couve de Murville,[4] a diplomatist whose whole training inclined him towards manoeuvre and manipulation, who was suddenly given the task of disrupting the Brussels negotiations. A current joke in Paris describes a high-level dinner party where everybody is deploring the alarming state of France's international relations, upon which M. Couve cuts in to observe "Ah! If only I were Foreign Minister!"

The General is beyond the reach of sentiment. During the long Algerian war the French Army and police, both in Metropolitan France and Algeria, made extensive use of torture to extract information, mostly from civilians, often from women. These methods began under the Fourth Republic, but when the General took over, his minister, André Malraux, said they would have to stop. Yet, despite violent protests (in which a niece of the General played a conspicuous part), the use of torture continued, and even increased, as the war dragged on. A group of objectors, mainly Catholics with special access to the Élysée, decided to ask the General to intervene. They chose as their spokesman a well-known French writer, a man who had himself suffered in Nazi concentration camps. The General received him and listened while he listed the evidence of what was happening and protested that these methods would ruin future relations between France and Algeria. Then the General interrupted. *"Le sang,"* he said, *"sèche vite"* (blood dries quickly).

Certainly de Gaulle himself has no time for pity. The explosion of an atom bomb over Hiroshima, for instance, caused many varied reactions. Some felt

[4] French Foreign Minister since 1958.—Ed.

that it was an intrinsically evil act. Others believed that it was justified since it shortened the war. De Gaulle heard the news with absolute calm: his only comment was that this would surely open the way for France to regain Indo-China. Sixteen years later, when France exploded its own first nuclear bomb, he sent the officers concerned one of the merriest messages this usually melancholy man has ever penned: "Hurrah for France! From this day she is stronger and prouder. . . ."

Ruse: The most conspicuous case of cunning and stealth in modern history is the story of how the General, after seeing his predecessors overthrown for allegedly contemplating peace negotiations in Algeria, took over power and gradually got the Army and the country to give the rebels everything they had ever been fighting for.

Contrary to a myth cultivated by the Gaullists, the General had not always believed in the independence of France's overseas possessions. He was himself in power in May 1945 when the first nationalist uprising in Algeria was suppressed. Two years after the event, French investigators revealed that some fifteen thousand Arab lives had been lost; a French Army General, reporting to the Senate on the events, said: "We regret having to say that groups of armed settlers were arrogating themselves the right to pass judgement and to execute. The government of the time [de Gaulle] by failing to punish these actions, was guilty of denying justice and truth to the people for whom it was responsible."

Reporting many years later on the seven-year Algerian war of independence, a Swiss journalist, Charles-Henri Favrod, wrote: "All the nationalists I met agreed on one thing: the revolution of 1954 (the year of the outbreak of the war which ended France's rule) was predetermined by the events of 1945. All the Nationalists I met at Cairo, Rome, Tunis, Bonn, Geneva, gave me hair-raising accounts of the massacres of those days and nights."

But during his long retirement at Colombey the General had come to terms with the idea that French withdrawal from Algeria was inevitable. A few weeks before returning to power in 1958 he received at his country home his war-time economic adviser, Georges Boris (uncle of the senior foreign office official, Olivier Wormser who was later to lead the French team in the Common Market negotiations with Britain), and told him that Algeria was moving inevitably towards independence. Back in office, de Gaulle's first task was to ensure Army loyalty; and soon he was holding wide his arms in Algeria and proclaiming: *"Je vous ai compris!"* to the cheering French settlers, who not unnaturally assumed he was going to be on their side. He subsequently offered *"la solution la plus française,"* which most people assumed meant keeping Algeria French (his supporters later pointed out that freedom and national independence were very French concepts).

Thus he played along the Army with a string of ambiguities, leaving everyone uncertain of his intentions. In May 1960 he visited Army camps dotted around Algeria and dined at the officers' messes. He told them that Algerian independence was "absurd" and "unthinkable," and the Algerians must become "fully-fledged Frenchmen" *(français à part entière)*. A year later he was still saying he would never discuss Algeria's future with cut-throats and rebels.

The Army were not the only ones whom de Gaulle deceived. While the war dragged on it remained official

French policy to secure Moslem cooperation; thus hundreds of thousands of Moslems, needing food and shelter, and apparently trusting the French promise that any new régime would give them a share in the country's political life, accepted French protection.

I cannot myself forget long arguments I used to have with a parachutist officer, Commander Saint-Marc, on the morality and wisdom of the integrationist policy by which the Army hoped to make Algerians full French citizens. Saint-Marc had himself fought in Indo-China and was appalled at having left so many Vietnamese who had worked with the French to be rounded up, mutilated, and killed by triumphant nationalists. Never again! he used to say— determined that in Algeria the Army would stay on and create a new modern state where the people would be safe,

social justice would be done, and France would use its resources and skill to combat hunger, illiteracy, and unemployment.

Then, suddenly, the General agreed to hand over the whole of Algeria to the FLN. Great concern has often and rightly been expressed at the U.N. and elsewhere over the appallingly high casualties among the Arab nationalists during the seven terrible years of war. But little is ever said by either side of the many thousands of friends of France who have subsequently died because they believed de Gaulle's promises. As for Saint-Marc, he is today in prison, charged with mutiny.

But Machiavelli was right: the Prince, after double-crossing everyone, was stronger at home and abroad than ever before.

ALEXANDER WERTH (1901–   ), for many years Paris correspondent for the *Manchester Guardian* and author of a series of books on twentieth-century France, criticizes d'Astier for exaggerating both de Gaulle's mystery and his "absurd" side. By contrast, Werth cites two strikingly appreciative descriptions of de Gaulle, by Winston Churchill and the renowned French novelist François Mauriac. He concludes that de Gaulle himself gave the clearest description of his motives and character in his book *The Edge of the Sword (Le Fil de l'épée)*, published in 1932.*

► Noble Anachronism

De Gaulle is a unique figure, the only monolithic figure in the recent history of France. Perhaps Stalin said at Yalta a truer word on de Gaulle than he fully realized: "De Gaulle—he is not complicated." In the highly complicated world of today statesmen generally reflect the complexity of their epoch. De Gaulle, on the contrary, with his single-track mind, with French Greatness as his *idée fixe*, is like an historical anachronism— a man who is not truly typical of mid-twentieth-century France.

In Volume IV of *The Second World War* Sir Winston Churchill wrote a striking page on de Gaulle; yet if this page is not as penetrating as it might be, is it not because Churchill, while instinctively detecting in de Gaulle certain qualities of greatness which were very similar to his own, perhaps failed to see that both his greatness and de Gaulle's were anchronistic? There was, however, this difference: while Churchill's "anachronism" turned out, for a variety of specifically British reasons, an almost miraculously successful one, de Gaulle's did not.

Both believed in "national greatness"; yet if this feeling of pride was stimulated in England by the ordeals of 1940, the greater disaster that befell France during the same year could only undermine her self-confidence. Throughout the war, Churchill and de Gaulle had to work on very different human material. The

---

* From Alexander Werth, *France, 1940–1955* (London: Robert Hale Ltd., 1956), pp. 201–207. Footnotes omitted.

victorious island could, five years later, still fancy itself a great power in the world; defeated France (for even in the midst of the Allied victory of 1945 she was still haunted by the memory of 1940) found it hard to believe in her own greatness. Perhaps the "logical" French mind was more aware than the sentimental British mind of the true distribution of strength in the world; perhaps also the fact that England was a "well-run" country, and France a "badly-run" country made a difference. If, in spite of everything, France still believed in her "superiority," this was different from "greatness," as de Gaulle understood it.

This is what Churchill wrote:

In these pages various severe statements based on events of the moment are set down about General de Gaulle, and certainly I had continuous difficulties and many sharp antagonisms with him. There was, however, a dominant element in our relationship. I could not regard him as representing active and prostrate France, nor indeed the France that had a right to decide freely the future for herself. I knew he was no friend of England. But I always recognized in him the spirit and conception which, across the pages of history, the word "France" would ever proclaim. I understood and admired, while I resented, his arrogant demeanour. Here he was—a refugee, an exile from his country under sentence of death, in a position entirely dependent upon the goodwill of the British Government, and also now of the United States. The Germans had conquered his country. He had no real foothold anywhere. Never mind: he defied all. Always, even when he was behaving worst, he seemed to express the personality of France—a great nation, with all its pride, authority and ambition. It was said in mockery that he thought himself the living representative of Joan of Arc. . . . This did not seem to me as absurd as it looked. Clemenceau, with whom it was said he also compared himself, was a

far wiser and more experienced statesman. But they both gave the same impression of being unconquerable Frenchmen.

This magnificent passage has, however, in its reference to France, the Churchillian fault of using too lightly sonorous and abstract words like "pride, authority, and ambition." Where was the France that was proud, authoritative, and ambitious? The words fit de Gaulle perfectly; but do they fit France —the *whole* of France, or even the greater part of it?

Nine years after his triumphal entry into Paris, de Gaulle was to say, looking back on it all:

Think by how many failures my public life has been marked! First I tried to persuade the civil and military authorities to endow France with an armoured force which would have spared us the invasion. I failed. After the disaster of 1940 I urged the Government, of which I was a member, to go to North Africa and evade the enemy. In vain. . . . I failed at Dakar. After victory I endeavoured to maintain the unity I had formed around myself. But this unity was broken. Later, in grave circumstances, I again tried, and failed. . . . If these failures had been mine, they would have been of no importance; but they were also the failures of France. True, from time to time, there were successes. . . . And yet—during the darkest moments of the war, I sometimes wondered: Perhaps it is my mission to represent in the history of our country its last upsurge toward the lofty heights. Perhaps it is my lot to have written the last pages in the book of our greatness.

And six months later, after another of de Gaulle's press conferences against EDC, Mauriac, who was there, felt what so many others must have felt: "the last Frenchman who had made his countrymen believe that they were still a great nation."

His words [wrote Mauriac] are like a cold

wind, coming from very far and very high, from the past when France was a great Nation. . . . Yes—he persuaded us of this at the darkest and most shameful moment of our history, and there are still millions of Frenchmen who have not forgotten it. . . . No one asked him: "Do you agree with the [Laniel] Government?" because by his very presence, General de Gaulle makes the dictatorship of Lilliput invisible to the naked eye. . . .

Mauriac also recalled that, at that same meeting, de Gaulle had used this strange phrase—and had used it naturally, almost without arrogance, but with a touch of melancholy pride: *"J'étais la France."* And no one had protested; because, in a sense, it was true. But only in a very limited sense. He symbolized during the years of the Occupation and Vichy, and for a short time after the Liberation the fighting spirit of a country that was predominantly pacifist and war-weary; he personified also a tradition of military honour in a country that was deeply conscious of its technical, military, economic—in short, its physical—inferiority. De Gaulle also carried the banner of national independence and national unity in a country that was conscious of having, in the main, been liberated by foreign armies, which was deeply divided, and which, not only militarily, but also economically was inclined to be increasingly dependent on stronger and wealthier nations.

De Gaulle had a large following on two occasions: when it was a case of driving out the German invaders, and when it was a case of preventing an (albeit hypothetical) Russian invasion. When the danger passed, he was forgotten by many; and he had only an insufficient following when he attempted a policy of genuine French independence and of *grandeur française*, and pro-

claimed that France would never be a pawn in the power politics of Russia and America.

As for home affairs, his—albeit unconscious—class loyalties were too strong, and he found no common language with the working-class. Also, he was proud, distant and austere; and if, at times, he was capable of uttering words of contempt or angry sarcasm, he lacked the boisterous wit of a Clemenceau or the lachrymose warmth of an Herriot, and expected hero-worship rather than popularity. His incapacity to make himself popular in a human way did much, in the early months of the Liberation, to estrange him from the Resistance.

Many people have known de Gaulle; countless articles and numerous books have been written about him—yet both to those who have known him, and, still more, to those who have written about him, he has never really "come alive." Some of his enemies in the London days —notably André Labarthe and Admiral Muselier—have spoken of his disloyalty, his low cunning, his capacity for intrigue; but even if, on occasion, he was disloyal, it could only have been in the name of some major political purpose (as he saw it); seldom, if ever, for any base or even plainly personal motive. If de Gaulle was deeply conscious of having a mission, he seems to have derived little *personal* pleasure from his triumphs, lacking completely the plebeian vanity of a Mussolini, a Hitler, or even a Napoleon.

One would think that, since he had political and military friends, they would tell us something of de Gaulle the Man, and bring out at least some warm, human touch in his character. But even in the two large tomes of Jacques Soustelle, one of his closest associates, one would look in vain for any-thing that seriously conflicts with the slightly caricatural portrait drawn of him by Emmanuel d'Astier, who served under him for a short time at Algiers as a member of the Liberation Commit-tee. . . .

[D'Astier's] is a cruel account of de Gaulle; and yet, as already said, the writers most favourable to him (includ-ing himself) add little to "humanize" him. What does one learn from them? That he was, before the war, a great military technician, that he had an ex-cellent record in the 1940 campaign but could, obviously, do no more than he did, all his advice on the organization of the French Army having been ignored; that he was the first to lead the revolt against the Armistice; that he fought a desperately hard diplomatic battle to get at least some recognition for him-self as the Symbol of Free France, this part of the story ending in the grand Paris apotheosis of August 1944.

But even to his closest followers he is something very like d'Astier's "Symbol." He is invariably *"le Général"*—tall, superior, and distant, and reminiscent of that historic anecdote he himself tells in *Le Fil de l'épée,* about somebody say-ing to Bonaparte as he stands before a noble and ancient monument: *"C'est triste."* To which Bonaparte replied: *"Oui, c'est triste comme la grandeur."*

My own limited acquaintance with de Gaulle suggests to me that d'Astier rather exaggerated his "absurd" side: for de Gaulle is sufficiently impressive to get away with even a little absurdity. But his lack of human warmth is, in-deed, disconcerting in a man of such powerful political emotions. Not that de Gaulle is "cold" in the ordinary sense; on the contrary, I would say that his "inhumanity" was a *warm inhuman-*

ity, like that of a great prince of the Church. The first volume of de Gaulle's *Mémoires,* published in 1954, bears out this impression, and is remarkably con-sistent with de Gaulle's writing twenty years earlier.

But was de Gaulle in reality quite as mysterious as d'Astier made him out to be? Eight years before the war, and two years before writing his famous *Vers l'armée de métier,* de Gaulle wrote a brilliant little essay which, read today, not only sounds truly prophetic, but very largely explains de Gaulle's char-acter and the workings of his mind. That de Gaulle had great erudition, a rare classical style of writing, and a su-perior mind is clearly revealed by *Le Fil de l'épée.* But it also reveals a vast superiority complex and almost certainly a faith in himself as a man of destiny. And it explains very clearly, eight years in advance, just *why* he "rebelled" in 1940. Character, Prestige, and a Doc-trine, according to de Gaulle, are the three main elements that make a great soldier and leader of men. And in all three chapters we find passages that look like X-rays of de Gaulle's own "mysteri-ous" mind.

The passion to act by one's self is ac-companied by a certain roughness. The man of character embodies the harshness inherent in his effort. His subordinates feel it, and often suffer from it. Such a chief is distant, because authority does not go without pres-tige, and prestige does not go without dis-tances being kept.

In relation to his superiors, he finds him-self in a difficult position. Sure of his own judgement and conscious of his strength, he makes no concessions to the desire to please. He . . . is not capable of passive obedience . . .

And then—this prophecy of 1940:

But when the danger becomes pressing . . . a kind of tidal wave sweeps a man of character right to the forefront. . . . And where, indeed, did one ever see a great human task being achieved without a man of character feeling the irresistible urge to act? . . . Nothing would have been achieved if counsels of base caution or suggestions of cowardly modesty had prevailed. More than that: those who do great things must *often ignore the conventions of a false discipline.* Thus in 1914 Lyautey kept Morocco despite orders from above; and after the battle of Jutland, Lord Fisher bitterly commented on Jellicoe's dispatches: "He has all Nelson's qualities, except one: he has not learned to disobey."

De Gaulle's "rebellion" of June 18 was no improvisation or sudden brainwave: he had prepared himself just for this kind of gesture many years before; his defiance of the Established Order in certain conditions had been thought out in advance. Similarly, in *Le Fil de l'épée,* in the chapter on Prestige, he explained the reasons why a great military leader must be reserved. "Nothing great was ever done in the midst of chatter," he wrote.

Hoche, general-in-chief at the age of twenty-four, and living in a world of rhetoric, nevertheless soon learned to be silent. His impetuous character and his brilliant oratory soon gave way to cold dignity and laconic speech. . . . And who was more taciturn than Bonaparte? . . . And the generals of the *Grande Armée* followed their master's example.

Alexander, Hannibal, Caesar, Richelieu, Condé, Hoche, Masséna, Napoleon —how de Gaulle loved to roll these names round his tongue! And to this member of a very narrow conservative military caste, the greatness of France and of the French Army was a kind of all-absorbing obsession; and no one was better prepared than he to assume in wartime the rôle of leader of the Free French.

So June 18 was not, as has sometimes been suggested, a lucky BBC fluke; psychologically, on the part of de Gaulle, it was a long-premeditated gesture. *Le Fil de l'épée* explains the de Gaulle of 1940; it also explains his haughtiness, his reserve, and even his decision to abandon power in January 1946, as we shall see later. For in 1946 he had to deal not with soldiers or potential soldiers, but with French civilians; and he was out of his element.

Suggested Reading

All study of de Gaulle should begin with his own writings, most of which have been translated into English. *The Edge of the Sword* (New York, 1960), originally published in 1932 as *Le Fil de l'épée,* contains his often-quoted analysis of the qualities of the man of character and the prerequisites for sustaining prestige. *The Army of the Future* (London, 1940), originally published in 1934 as *Vers l'armée de métier,* gives his recommendation for the creation of a tank force of six divisions, as well as a superb description of the geography of northeastern France, showing Paris open to invasion—Paris, "monument, market, factory, union of a thousand arteries, surrounded by quickly penetrated forests, lacking any acropolis, a prey so near, so beautiful and so easy!" His speeches during the war years are collected in *The Speeches of General de Gaulle* (Oxford, 1944) and those during the RPF in *La France sera la France: Ce que veut Charles de Gaulle* (Paris, 1951). His principal pronouncements since 1958, including the indispensable press conferences, are given in French Embassy Press and Information Division, New York, *Major Addresses, Statements and Press Conferences of General Charles de Gaulle, May 19, 1958–January 31, 1964* (New York, 1965). To these should be added E. Mignon, *Les Mots du Général* (Paris, 1962), and André Passeron's *De Gaulle parle* (Paris, 1962), which includes the telling asides de Gaulle deliberately lets slip at gatherings of newsmen, parliamentarians, or provincial notables in the Elysée Palace. Finally, there are the supremely important and impressive *War Memoirs* (New York, 1955–1960), although one might temper one's judgment by reading General Maxime Weygand's critique, *En lisant les Mémoires du Général de Gaulle* (Paris, 1955), Alfred Fabre-Luce, *Le Plus illustre des Français* (Paris, 1961), pp. 169–186, and Jean-François Revel's analysis of de Gaulle's character as revealed through his style in *Le Style du Général* (Paris, 1959).

De Gaulle's early career is thoroughly covered in most of the biographies. Georges Cattaui's *Charles de Gaulle: L'Homme et son destin* (Paris, 1960), gives a good description of his family background; Philippe Barrès *Charles de Gaulle* (Garden City, N. Y., 1941) presents him as a military genius; his boyhood friend, Louis Nachin, in *Charles de Gaulle: Général de France* (Paris, 1944) includes, among other personal sidelights, the letter of 1928 in which de Gaulle prophesied, "in a few years they will be hanging onto my coat-tails to save the country." English admirers like Duncan Grinnell-Milne, *The Triumph of Integrity: A Portrait of Charles de Gaulle* (London, 1961) and Edward Ashcroft, *De Gaulle* (London, 1962) show that Gaullism is not a purely French phenomenon.

De Gaulle's wartime relations with his allies have roused a good deal of curiosity recently. On his relations with Roosevelt, one should read Arthur Layton Funk's *Charles de Gaulle: The Crucial Years, 1943–1944* (Norman, Okla., 1959) and Milton Viorst, *Hostile Allies: F.D.R. and de Gaulle* (New York, 1965). An objective personal appraisal is perhaps possible after reading Cordell Hull, *Memoirs* (New York, 1948), Admiral Leahy's *I Was There* (New York, 1950), and Robert E. Sherwood, *Roosevelt and Hopkins* (New York, 1950), for the American side; Winston S. Churchill, *The Second World War* (Boston, 1948–1953), especially Vol. 4, p. 611, and Duff Cooper's *Old Men Forget* (New York, 1954), for the British side; and Jacques Soustelle's *Envers et contre tout* (Paris, 1947) and General Georges Catroux's *Dans la bataille de Méditerranée* (Paris, 1949), and General Henri Giraud, *Une Seul victoire* (Paris, 1949), and perhaps the vehemently anti-Gaullist book of Henri de Kerillis, *I Accuse de Gaulle* (New York, 1946), for the French.

The glorious return to France is chronicled in Robert Aron's *De Gaulle Before Paris: The Liberation of France, June–August 1944* (London, 1962) and *De Gaulle Triumphant: The Liberation of France, August 1944–May 1945* (London, 1963) and Adrien Dansette's *Histoire de la libération de Paris* (Paris, 1946). Marshal Jean de Lattre de Tassigny's *The History of the French First Army* (London, 1952) details the campaigns of the Army of Rhine and Danube, and provides some revealing insights into de Gaulle's conception of the French role in the invasion of Germany. De Gaulle's policy as premier, 1944–1946, is described in Alexander Werth, *France, 1940–1955* (New York, 1956), Dorothy Pickles, *French Politics: The First Years of the Fourth Republic* (London, 1953), and Jacques Fauvet, *Les Forces politiques en France* (Paris, 1951) and *La IVe République* (Paris, 1959). The best description of de Gaulle's foreign policy aims is given in Alfred Grosser's *La Politique étrangère de la IVe République* (Paris, 1961). Grosser has also given an account of the foreign policy of the Fifth Republic: *La Politique étrangère de la Ve République* (Paris, 1965).

The RPF receives only passing notice in most books. The best summary is probably that of Philip M. Williams, in *Crisis and Compromise: Politics in the Fourth Republic* (Hamden, Conn., 1964).

The events of May 13–June 1, 1958, have been much publicized, without much light being thrown on de Gaulle's personal share. The most reliable accounts of events in Algeria are Serge and Merry Bromberger's *Les 13 complots du 13 mai* (Paris, 1959) and Jean-Raymond Tournoux's *Secrets d'état* (Paris, 1960). The attitude in France to de Gaulle's return is described in Léo Hamon's *De Gaulle dans la République* (Paris, 1958)

and Alexander Werth, *The De Gaulle Revolution* (London, 1960).

The constitution and political character of the Fifth Republic are discussed in Dorothy Pickles, *The Fifth French Republic* (New York, 1962); Nicholas Wahl, *The Fifth Republic: France's New Political System* (New York, 1959); Philip M. Williams and Martin Harrison, *De Gaulle's Republic* (London, 1961); Roy C. Macridis and Bernard E. Brown, *The De Gaulle Republic* (Homewood, Ill., 1960); and Maurice Duverger, *La Ve République* (Paris, 1959). The monarchial style of the new regime has provided material for France's satirists, especially for André Ribaud's weekly chronicle of the court in *Le Canard enchaîné*, which has been published as *La Cour: Chronique du royaume* (Paris, 1961) and for the penetrating Michelin-style guide to the leading Gaullists by Pierre Viansson-Ponté, *The King and His Court* (Boston, 1964).

De Gaulle's attempts to find a solution to the Algerian problem are analyzed in William G. Andrews, *French Politics and Algeria: The Process of Policy Formation, 1954–1962* (New York, 1962), and by Dorothy Pickles, *Algeria and France: From Colonialism to Co-operation* (New York, 1963). Serge and Merry Bromberger, Jean-François Chauvel, and Georgette Elgey describe the revolt of the European Algerians of January 21–February 1, 1960, in *Barricades et colonels* (Paris, 1960); Jacques Fauvet and Jean Planchais, the generals' revolt of April 22–26, 1961, in *La Fronde des généraux* (Paris, 1961). Jacques Soustelle's disappointment with his former hero's Algerian policy is expressed in *L'Espérance trahie* (Paris, 1962). The feeling that they had been betrayed by de Gaulle is dominant in the trials of Generals Salan, Jouhaud, Challe, and Zeller, verbatim reports of which are given in *Le Procès de Raoul Salan* (Paris, 1962), *Le Procès d'Edmond Jouhaud* (Paris, 1962), and *Les Procès des Généraux Challe et Zeller* (Paris, 1961). James H. Meisel's lively *The Fall of the Republic: Military Revolt in France* (Ann Arbor, Mich., 1962) studies the French army

ST. MARY'S COLLEGE OF MARYLAND
ST. MARY'S CITY, MARYLAND 20686

as a "political army which develops its own ideology of power"; Edgar S. Furniss's *De Gaulle and the French Army: A Crisis in Civil-Military Relations* (New York, 1964) describes the positive role de Gaulle envisioned for the army, when freed of the Algerian imbroglio, as "an effective instrument for his statecraft." This conception necessarily involves, at enormous cost, possession of the atomic bomb. The wisdom of such a policy is challenged in Raymond Aron's *Le Grand débat* (Paris, 1963), and supported in Alexandre Sanguinetti's *La France et l'arme atomique* (Paris, 1963).

De Gaulle's European policy has provoked a number of protests. Roger Massip, *De Gaulle et l'Europe* (Paris, 1963) is fairly restrained; Paul Reynaud's *The Foreign Policy of Charles de Gaulle* (New York, 1964) is vehement. The policy of reconciliation of Teuton and Gaul is described in F. Roy Willis, *France, Germany and the New Europe, 1945–1963* (Stanford, Calif., 1965), which also details de Gaulle's aims for the European Community. The veto of British entry in the Common Market prompted a series of analyses of de Gaulle's motives, of which the most vigorous are Nora Beloff's *The General Says No* (London, 1963) and John Pinder, *Europe against de Gaulle* (New York, 1963), and the most judicious and detailed is Miriam Camps, *Britain and the European Community, 1955–1963* (Princeton, N.J., 1964).